CPACE Written

SECRETS

Study Guide

Your Key to Exam Success

CPACE Test Review for the
California Preliminary Administrative
Credential Examination

Dear Future Exam Success Story:

First of all, **THANK YOU** for purchasing Mometrix study materials!

Second, congratulations! You are one of the few determined test-takers who are committed to doing whatever it takes to excel on your exam. **You have come to the right place.** We developed these study materials with one goal in mind: to deliver you the information you need in a format that's concise and easy to use.

In addition to optimizing your guide for the content of the test, we've outlined our recommended steps for breaking down the preparation process into small, attainable goals so you can make sure you stay on track.

We've also analyzed the entire test-taking process, identifying the most common pitfalls and showing how you can overcome them and be ready for any curveball the test throws you.

Standardized testing is one of the biggest obstacles on your road to success, which only increases the importance of doing well in the high-pressure, high-stakes environment of test day. Your results on this test could have a significant impact on your future, and this guide provides the information and practical advice to help you achieve your full potential on test day.

Your success is our success

We would love to hear from you! If you would like to share the story of your exam success or if you have any questions or comments in regard to our products, please contact us at **800-673-8175** or **support@mometrix.com**.

Thanks again for your business and we wish you continued success!

Sincerely,
The Mometrix Test Preparation Team

Need more help? Check out our flashcards at: http://MometrixFlashcards.com/CSET

Written and edited by the Mometrix Exam Secrets Test Prep Team
Printed in the United States of America

TABLE OF CONTENTS

INTRODUCTION 1

SECRET KEY #1 – PLAN BIG, STUDY SMALL 2
- Information Organization 2
- Time Management 2
- Study Environment 2

SECRET KEY #2 – MAKE YOUR STUDYING COUNT 3
- Retention 3
- Modality 3

SECRET KEY #3 – PRACTICE THE RIGHT WAY 4
- Practice Test Strategy 5

SECRET KEY #4 – PACE YOURSELF 6

SECRET KEY #5 – HAVE A PLAN FOR GUESSING 7
- When to Start the Guessing Process 7
- How to Narrow Down the Choices 8
- Which Answer to Choose 9

TEST-TAKING STRATEGIES 10
- Question Strategies 10
- Answer Choice Strategies 11
- General Strategies 12
- Final Notes 13

VISIONARY LEADERSHIP 15

INSTRUCTIONAL LEADERSHIP 29

SCHOOL IMPROVEMENT LEADERSHIP 40

PROFESSIONAL LEARNING AND GROWTH LEADERSHIP 57

ORGANIZATIONAL AND SYSTEMS LEADERSHIP 69

COMMUNITY LEADERSHIP 94

CPACE PRACTICE TEST 102

ANSWERS AND EXPLANATIONS 122

HOW TO OVERCOME TEST ANXIETY 137
- Causes of Test Anxiety 137
- Elements of Test Anxiety 138
- Effects of Test Anxiety 138
- Physical Steps for Beating Test Anxiety 139
- Mental Steps for Beating Test Anxiety 140
- Study Strategy 141
- Test Tips 143
- Important Qualification 144

THANK YOU 145

ADDITIONAL BONUS MATERIAL 146

Introduction

Thank you for purchasing this resource! You have made the choice to prepare yourself for a test that could have a huge impact on your future, and this guide is designed to help you be fully ready for test day. Obviously, it's important to have a solid understanding of the test material, but you also need to be prepared for the unique environment and stressors of the test, so that you can perform to the best of your abilities.

For this purpose, the first section that appears in this guide is the **Secret Keys**. We've devoted countless hours to meticulously researching what works and what doesn't, and we've boiled down our findings to the five most impactful steps you can take to improve your performance on the test. We start at the beginning with study planning and move through the preparation process, all the way to the testing strategies that will help you get the most out of what you know when you're finally sitting in front of the test.

We recommend that you start preparing for your test as far in advance as possible. However, if you've bought this guide as a last-minute study resource and only have a few days before your test, we recommend that you skip over the first two Secret Keys since they address a long-term study plan.

If you struggle with **test anxiety**, we strongly encourage you to check out our recommendations for how you can overcome it. Test anxiety is a formidable foe, but it can be beaten, and we want to make sure you have the tools you need to defeat it.

Secret Key #1 – Plan Big, Study Small

There's a lot riding on your performance. If you want to ace this test, you're going to need to keep your skills sharp and the material fresh in your mind. You need a plan that lets you review everything you need to know while still fitting in your schedule. We'll break this strategy down into three categories.

Information Organization

Start with the information you already have: the official test outline. From this, you can make a complete list of all the concepts you need to cover before the test. Organize these concepts into groups that can be studied together, and create a list of any related vocabulary you need to learn so you can brush up on any difficult terms. You'll want to keep this vocabulary list handy once you actually start studying since you may need to add to it along the way.

Time Management

Once you have your set of study concepts, decide how to spread them out over the time you have left before the test. Break your study plan into small, clear goals so you have a manageable task for each day and know exactly what you're doing. Then just focus on one small step at a time. When you manage your time this way, you don't need to spend hours at a time studying. Studying a small block of content for a short period each day helps you retain information better and avoid stressing over how much you have left to do. You can relax knowing that you have a plan to cover everything in time. In order for this strategy to be effective though, you have to start studying early and stick to your schedule. Avoid the exhaustion and futility that comes from last-minute cramming!

Study Environment

The environment you study in has a big impact on your learning. Studying in a coffee shop, while probably more enjoyable, is not likely to be as fruitful as studying in a quiet room. It's important to keep distractions to a minimum. You're only planning to study for a short block of time, so make the most of it. Don't pause to check your phone or get up to find a snack. It's also important to **avoid multitasking**. Research has consistently shown that multitasking will make your studying dramatically less effective. Your study area should also be comfortable and well-lit so you don't have the distraction of straining your eyes or sitting on an uncomfortable chair.

The time of day you study is also important. You want to be rested and alert. Don't wait until just before bedtime. Study when you'll be most likely to comprehend and remember. Even better, if you know what time of day your test will be, set that time aside for study. That way your brain will be used to working on that subject at that specific time and you'll have a better chance of recalling information.

Finally, it can be helpful to team up with others who are studying for the same test. Your actual studying should be done in as isolated an environment as possible, but the work of organizing the information and setting up the study plan can be divided up. In between study sessions, you can discuss with your teammates the concepts that you're all studying and quiz each other on the details. Just be sure that your teammates are as serious about the test as you are. If you find that your study time is being replaced with social time, you might need to find a new team.

Secret Key #2 – Make Your Studying Count

You're devoting a lot of time and effort to preparing for this test, so you want to be absolutely certain it will pay off. This means doing more than just reading the content and hoping you can remember it on test day. It's important to make every minute of study count. There are two main areas you can focus on to make your studying count:

Retention

It doesn't matter how much time you study if you can't remember the material. You need to make sure you are retaining the concepts. To check your retention of the information you're learning, try recalling it at later times with minimal prompting. Try carrying around flashcards and glance at one or two from time to time or ask a friend who's also studying for the test to quiz you.

To enhance your retention, look for ways to put the information into practice so that you can apply it rather than simply recalling it. If you're using the information in practical ways, it will be much easier to remember. Similarly, it helps to solidify a concept in your mind if you're not only reading it to yourself but also explaining it to someone else. Ask a friend to let you teach them about a concept you're a little shaky on (or speak aloud to an imaginary audience if necessary). As you try to summarize, define, give examples, and answer your friend's questions, you'll understand the concepts better and they will stay with you longer. Finally, step back for a big picture view and ask yourself how each piece of information fits with the whole subject. When you link the different concepts together and see them working together as a whole, it's easier to remember the individual components.

Finally, practice showing your work on any multi-step problems, even if you're just studying. Writing out each step you take to solve a problem will help solidify the process in your mind, and you'll be more likely to remember it during the test.

Modality

Modality simply refers to the means or method by which you study. Choosing a study modality that fits your own individual learning style is crucial. No two people learn best in exactly the same way, so it's important to know your strengths and use them to your advantage.

For example, if you learn best by visualization, focus on visualizing a concept in your mind and draw an image or a diagram. Try color-coding your notes, illustrating them, or creating symbols that will trigger your mind to recall a learned concept. If you learn best by hearing or discussing information, find a study partner who learns the same way or read aloud to yourself. Think about how to put the information in your own words. Imagine that you are giving a lecture on the topic and record yourself so you can listen to it later.

For any learning style, flashcards can be helpful. Organize the information so you can take advantage of spare moments to review. Underline key words or phrases. Use different colors for different categories. Mnemonic devices (such as creating a short list in which every item starts with the same letter) can also help with retention. Find what works best for you and use it to store the information in your mind most effectively and easily.

Secret Key #3 – Practice the Right Way

Your success on test day depends not only on how many hours you put into preparing, but also on whether you prepared the right way. It's good to check along the way to see if your studying is paying off. One of the most effective ways to do this is by taking practice tests to evaluate your progress. Practice tests are useful because they show exactly where you need to improve. Every time you take a practice test, pay special attention to these three groups of questions:

- The questions you got wrong
- The questions you had to guess on, even if you guessed right
- The questions you found difficult or slow to work through

This will show you exactly what your weak areas are, and where you need to devote more study time. Ask yourself why each of these questions gave you trouble. Was it because you didn't understand the material? Was it because you didn't remember the vocabulary? Do you need more repetitions on this type of question to build speed and confidence? Dig into those questions and figure out how you can strengthen your weak areas as you go back to review the material.

Additionally, many practice tests have a section explaining the answer choices. It can be tempting to read the explanation and think that you now have a good understanding of the concept. However, an explanation likely only covers part of the question's broader context. Even if the explanation makes sense, **go back and investigate** every concept related to the question until you're positive you have a thorough understanding.

As you go along, keep in mind that the practice test is just that: practice. Memorizing these questions and answers will not be very helpful on the actual test because it is unlikely to have any of the same exact questions. If you only know the right answers to the sample questions, you won't be prepared for the real thing. **Study the concepts** until you understand them fully, and then you'll be able to answer any question that shows up on the test.

It's important to wait on the practice tests until you're ready. If you take a test on your first day of study, you may be overwhelmed by the amount of material covered and how much you need to learn. Work up to it gradually.

On test day, you'll need to be prepared for answering questions, managing your time, and using the test-taking strategies you've learned. It's a lot to balance, like a mental marathon that will have a big impact on your future. Like training for a marathon, you'll need to start slowly and work your way up. When test day arrives, you'll be ready.

Start with the strategies you've read in the first two Secret Keys—plan your course and study in the way that works best for you. If you have time, consider using multiple study resources to get different approaches to the same concepts. It can be helpful to see difficult concepts from more than one angle. Then find a good source for practice tests. Many times, the test website will suggest potential study resources or provide sample tests.

Practice Test Strategy

When you're ready to start taking practice tests, follow this strategy:

Untimed and Open-Book Practice

Take the first test with no time constraints and with your notes and study guide handy. Take your time and focus on applying the strategies you've learned.

Timed and Open-Book Practice

Take the second practice test open-book as well, but set a timer and practice pacing yourself to finish in time.

Timed and Closed-Book Practice

Take any other practice tests as if it were test day. Set a timer and put away your study materials. Sit at a table or desk in a quiet room, imagine yourself at the testing center, and answer questions as quickly and accurately as possible.

Keep repeating timed and closed-book tests on a regular basis until you run out of practice tests or it's time for the actual test. Your mind will be ready for the schedule and stress of test day, and you'll be able to focus on recalling the material you've learned.

Secret Key #4 – Pace Yourself

Once you're fully prepared for the material on the test, your biggest challenge on test day will be managing your time. Just knowing that the clock is ticking can make you panic even if you have plenty of time left. Work on pacing yourself so you can build confidence against the time constraints of the exam. Pacing is a difficult skill to master, especially in a high-pressure environment, so **practice is vital**.

Set time expectations for your pace based on how much time is available. For example, if a section has 60 questions and the time limit is 30 minutes, you know you have to average 30 seconds or less per question in order to answer them all. Although 30 seconds is the hard limit, set 25 seconds per question as your goal, so you reserve extra time to spend on harder questions. When you budget extra time for the harder questions, you no longer have any reason to stress when those questions take longer to answer.

Don't let this time expectation distract you from working through the test at a calm, steady pace, but keep it in mind so you don't spend too much time on any one question. Recognize that taking extra time on one question you don't understand may keep you from answering two that you do understand later in the test. If your time limit for a question is up and you're still not sure of the answer, mark it and move on, and come back to it later if the time and the test format allow. If the testing format doesn't allow you to return to earlier questions, just make an educated guess; then put it out of your mind and move on.

On the easier questions, be careful not to rush. It may seem wise to hurry through them so you have more time for the challenging ones, but it's not worth missing one if you know the concept and just didn't take the time to read the question fully. Work efficiently but make sure you understand the question and have looked at all of the answer choices, since more than one may seem right at first.

Even if you're paying attention to the time, you may find yourself a little behind at some point. You should speed up to get back on track, but do so wisely. Don't panic; just take a few seconds less on each question until you're caught up. Don't guess without thinking, but do look through the answer choices and eliminate any you know are wrong. If you can get down to two choices, it is often worthwhile to guess from those. Once you've chosen an answer, move on and don't dwell on any that you skipped or had to hurry through. If a question was taking too long, chances are it was one of the harder ones, so you weren't as likely to get it right anyway.

On the other hand, if you find yourself getting ahead of schedule, it may be beneficial to slow down a little. The more quickly you work, the more likely you are to make a careless mistake that will affect your score. You've budgeted time for each question, so don't be afraid to spend that time. Practice an efficient but careful pace to get the most out of the time you have.

Secret Key #5 – Have a Plan for Guessing

When you're taking the test, you may find yourself stuck on a question. Some of the answer choices seem better than others, but you don't see the one answer choice that is obviously correct. What do you do?

The scenario described above is very common, yet most test takers have not effectively prepared for it. Developing and practicing a plan for guessing may be one of the single most effective uses of your time as you get ready for the exam.

In developing your plan for guessing, there are three questions to address:

- When should you start the guessing process?
- How should you narrow down the choices?
- Which answer should you choose?

When to Start the Guessing Process

Unless your plan for guessing is to select C every time (which, despite its merits, is not what we recommend), you need to leave yourself enough time to apply your answer elimination strategies. Since you have a limited amount of time for each question, that means that if you're going to give yourself the best shot at guessing correctly, you have to decide quickly whether or not you will guess.

Of course, the best-case scenario is that you don't have to guess at all, so first, see if you can answer the question based on your knowledge of the subject and basic reasoning skills. Focus on the key words in the question and try to jog your memory of related topics. Give yourself a chance to bring the knowledge to mind, but once you realize that you don't have (or you can't access) the knowledge you need to answer the question, it's time to start the guessing process.

It's almost always better to start the guessing process too early than too late. It only takes a few seconds to remember something and answer the question from knowledge. Carefully eliminating wrong answer choices takes longer. Plus, going through the process of eliminating answer choices can actually help jog your memory.

Summary: Start the guessing process as soon as you decide that you can't answer the question based on your knowledge.

How to Narrow Down the Choices

The next chapter in this book (**Test-Taking Strategies**) includes a wide range of strategies for how to approach questions and how to look for answer choices to eliminate. You will definitely want to read those carefully, practice them, and figure out which ones work best for you. Here though, we're going to address a mindset rather than a particular strategy.

Your chances of guessing an answer correctly depend on how many options you are choosing from.

How many choices you have	How likely you are to guess correctly
5	20%
4	25%
3	33%
2	50%
1	100%

You can see from this chart just how valuable it is to be able to eliminate incorrect answers and make an educated guess, but there are two things that many test takers do that cause them to miss out on the benefits of guessing:

- Accidentally eliminating the correct answer
- Selecting an answer based on an impression

We'll look at the first one here, and the second one in the next section.

To avoid accidentally eliminating the correct answer, we recommend a thought exercise called **the $5 challenge**. In this challenge, you only eliminate an answer choice from contention if you are willing to bet $5 on it being wrong. Why $5? Five dollars is a small but not insignificant amount of money. It's an amount you could afford to lose but wouldn't want to throw away. And while losing $5 once might not hurt too much, doing it twenty times will set you back $100. In the same way, each small decision you make—eliminating a choice here, guessing on a question there—won't by itself impact your score very much, but when you put them all together, they can make a big difference. By holding each answer choice elimination decision to a higher standard, you can reduce the risk of accidentally eliminating the correct answer.

The $5 challenge can also be applied in a positive sense: If you are willing to bet $5 that an answer choice *is* correct, go ahead and mark it as correct.

Summary: Only eliminate an answer choice if you are willing to bet $5 that it is wrong.

Which Answer to Choose

You're taking the test. You've run into a hard question and decided you'll have to guess. You've eliminated all the answer choices you're willing to bet $5 on. Now you have to pick an answer. Why do we even need to talk about this? Why can't you just pick whichever one you feel like when the time comes?

The answer to these questions is that if you don't come into the test with a plan, you'll rely on your impression to select an answer choice, and if you do that, you risk falling into a trap. The test writers know that everyone who takes their test will be guessing on some of the questions, so they intentionally write wrong answer choices to seem plausible. You still have to pick an answer though, and if the wrong answer choices are designed to look right, how can you ever be sure that you're not falling for their trap? The best solution we've found to this dilemma is to take the decision out of your hands entirely. Here is the process we recommend:

Once you've eliminated any choices that you are confident (willing to bet $5) are wrong, select the first remaining choice as your answer.

Whether you choose to select the first remaining choice, the second, or the last, the important thing is that you use some preselected standard. Using this approach guarantees that you will not be enticed into selecting an answer choice that looks right, because you are not basing your decision on how the answer choices look.

This is not meant to make you question your knowledge. Instead, it is to help you recognize the difference between your knowledge and your impressions. There's a huge difference between thinking an answer is right because of what you know, and thinking an answer is right because it looks or sounds like it should be right.

Summary: To ensure that your selection is appropriately random, make a predetermined selection from among all answer choices you have not eliminated.

Test-Taking Strategies

This section contains a list of test-taking strategies that you may find helpful as you work through the test. By taking what you know and applying logical thought, you can maximize your chances of answering any question correctly!

It is very important to realize that every question is different and every person is different: no single strategy will work on every question, and no single strategy will work for every person. That's why we've included all of them here, so you can try them out and determine which ones work best for different types of questions and which ones work best for you.

Question Strategies

Read Carefully

Read the question and answer choices carefully. Don't miss the question because you misread the terms. You have plenty of time to read each question thoroughly and make sure you understand what is being asked. Yet a happy medium must be attained, so don't waste too much time. You must read carefully, but efficiently.

Contextual Clues

Look for contextual clues. If the question includes a word you are not familiar with, look at the immediate context for some indication of what the word might mean. Contextual clues can often give you all the information you need to decipher the meaning of an unfamiliar word. Even if you can't determine the meaning, you may be able to narrow down the possibilities enough to make a solid guess at the answer to the question.

Prefixes

If you're having trouble with a word in the question or answer choices, try dissecting it. Take advantage of every clue that the word might include. Prefixes and suffixes can be a huge help. Usually they allow you to determine a basic meaning. Pre- means before, post- means after, pro - is positive, de- is negative. From prefixes and suffixes, you can get an idea of the general meaning of the word and try to put it into context.

Hedge Words

Watch out for critical hedge words, such as *likely*, *may*, *can*, *sometimes*, *often*, *almost*, *mostly*, *usually*, *generally*, *rarely*, and *sometimes*. Question writers insert these hedge phrases to cover every possibility. Often an answer choice will be wrong simply because it leaves no room for exception. Be on guard for answer choices that have definitive words such as *exactly* and *always*.

Switchback Words

Stay alert for *switchbacks*. These are the words and phrases frequently used to alert you to shifts in thought. The most common switchback words are *but*, *although*, and *however*. Others include *nevertheless, on the other hand, even though, while, in spite of, despite, regardless of*. Switchback words are important to catch because they can change the direction of the question or an answer choice.

Face Value

When in doubt, use common sense. Accept the situation in the problem at face value. Don't read too much into it. These problems will not require you to make wild assumptions. If you have to go beyond creativity and warp time or space in order to have an answer choice fit the question, then you should move on and consider the other answer choices. These are normal problems rooted in reality. The applicable relationship or explanation may not be readily apparent, but it is there for you to figure out. Use your common sense to interpret anything that isn't clear.

Answer Choice Strategies

Answer Selection

The most thorough way to pick an answer choice is to identify and eliminate wrong answers until only one is left, then confirm it is the correct answer. Sometimes an answer choice may immediately seem right, but be careful. The test writers will usually put more than one reasonable answer choice on each question, so take a second to read all of them and make sure that the other choices are not equally obvious. As long as you have time left, it is better to read every answer choice than to pick the first one that looks right without checking the others.

Answer Choice Families

An answer choice family consists of two (in rare cases, three) answer choices that are very similar in construction and cannot all be true at the same time. If you see two answer choices that are direct opposites or parallels, one of them is usually the correct answer. For instance, if one answer choice says that quantity x increases and another either says that quantity x decreases (opposite) or says that quantity y increases (parallel), then those answer choices would fall into the same family. An answer choice that doesn't match the construction of the answer choice family is more likely to be incorrect. Most questions will not have answer choice families, but when they do appear, you should be prepared to recognize them.

Eliminate Answers

Eliminate answer choices as soon as you realize they are wrong, but make sure you consider all possibilities. If you are eliminating answer choices and realize that the last one you are left with is also wrong, don't panic. Start over and consider each choice again. There may be something you missed the first time that you will realize on the second pass.

Avoid Fact Traps

Don't be distracted by an answer choice that is factually true but doesn't answer the question. You are looking for the choice that answers the question. Stay focused on what the question is asking for so you don't accidentally pick an answer that is true but incorrect. Always go back to the question and make sure the answer choice you've selected actually answers the question and is not merely a true statement.

Extreme Statements

In general, you should avoid answers that put forth extreme actions as standard practice or proclaim controversial ideas as established fact. An answer choice that states the "process should be used in certain situations, if..." is much more likely to be correct than one that states the "process should be discontinued completely." The first is a calm rational statement and doesn't even make a definitive, uncompromising stance, using a hedge word *if* to provide wiggle room, whereas the second choice is a radical idea and far more extreme.

Benchmark

As you read through the answer choices and you come across one that seems to answer the question well, mentally select that answer choice. This is not your final answer, but it's the one that will help you evaluate the other answer choices. The one that you selected is your benchmark or standard for judging each of the other answer choices. Every other answer choice must be compared to your benchmark. That choice is correct until proven otherwise by another answer choice beating it. If you find a better answer, then that one becomes your new benchmark. Once you've decided that no other choice answers the question as well as your benchmark, you have your final answer.

Predict the Answer

Before you even start looking at the answer choices, it is often best to try to predict the answer. When you come up with the answer on your own, it is easier to avoid distractions and traps because you will know exactly what to look for. The right answer choice is unlikely to be word-for-word what you came up with, but it should be a close match. Even if you are confident that you have the right answer, you should still take the time to read each option before moving on.

General Strategies

Tough Questions

If you are stumped on a problem or it appears too hard or too difficult, don't waste time. Move on! Remember though, if you can quickly check for obviously incorrect answer choices, your chances of guessing correctly are greatly improved. Before you completely give up, at least try to knock out a couple of possible answers. Eliminate what you can and then guess at the remaining answer choices before moving on.

Check Your Work

Since you will probably not know every term listed and the answer to every question, it is important that you get credit for the ones that you do know. Don't miss any questions through careless mistakes. If at all possible, try to take a second to look back over your answer selection and make sure you've selected the correct answer choice and haven't made a costly careless mistake (such as marking an answer choice that you didn't mean to mark). This quick double check should more than pay for itself in caught mistakes for the time it costs.

Pace Yourself

It's easy to be overwhelmed when you're looking at a page full of questions; your mind is confused and full of random thoughts, and the clock is ticking down faster than you would like. Calm down and maintain the pace that you have set for yourself. Especially as you get down to the last few minutes of the test, don't let the small numbers on the clock make you panic. As long as you are on track by monitoring your pace, you are guaranteed to have time for each question.

Don't Rush

It is very easy to make errors when you are in a hurry. Maintaining a fast pace in answering questions is pointless if it makes you miss questions that you would have gotten right otherwise. Test writers like to include distracting information and wrong answers that seem right. Taking a little extra time to avoid careless mistakes can make all the difference in your test score. Find a pace that allows you to be confident in the answers that you select.

Keep Moving

Panicking will not help you pass the test, so do your best to stay calm and keep moving. Taking deep breaths and going through the answer elimination steps you practiced can help to break through a stress barrier and keep your pace.

Final Notes

The combination of a solid foundation of content knowledge and the confidence that comes from practicing your plan for applying that knowledge is the key to maximizing your performance on test day. As your foundation of content knowledge is built up and strengthened, you'll find that the strategies included in this chapter become more and more effective in helping you quickly sift through the distractions and traps of the test to isolate the correct answer.

Now it's time to move on to the test content chapters of this book, but be sure to keep your goal in mind. As you read, think about how you will be able to apply this information on the test. If you've already seen sample questions for the test and you have an idea of the question format and style, try to come up with questions of your own that you can answer based on what you're reading. This will give you valuable practice applying your knowledge in the same ways you can expect to on test day.

Good luck and good studying!

Visionary Leadership

Creating a Culture of Learning

A culture of learning is an environment with an emphasis on learning and a high expectation for academic achievement. It involves intellectual stimulation for students, staff, and leadership. Evidence of a culture of learning includes implementing effective classroom instructional strategies for student learning, implementing processes of continuous improvement to increase student learning and academic performance, participating in professional development for teachers and staff collectively and individually, and the acquiring and sharing of knowledge by leadership. When a culture of learning is present, school leaders seek ways to support the learning needs of all students so all can be academically successful. School leaders also seek ways to support the learning needs of teachers and staff to assist them in their professional growth.

Developing a Culture of Learning

To develop a culture of learning on campus, a school leader must consider this culture in all decision making. First, the school should be designed in a way that facilitates a culture of learning. This means that there are sufficient learning spaces to accommodate a variety of learning strategies, along with furniture and resources that support those learning spaces. For example, there should be a library resource center with appropriate shelving, books, and technology resources. A school leader must also hire and train staff in a way that supports a culture of learning. Candidates for hire that do not support a culture of learning should not be selected. The leader must also communicate expectations for a culture of learning to staff, students, parents, and community stakeholders to ensure that everyone is aware of the expectations. When possible, the leader can support the school's culture by encouraging families to develop their own culture of learning and providing the resources and support for them to do so. For example, the leader may give books to families to encourage reading in the home.

Supporting a Culture of Learning

School Vision

The school vision serves as a guide and a foundation for all strategic planning and communicates the purpose and focus of the school to all stakeholders. One of the goals of a school leader is to create a culture of learning on campus. Including this concept in the school vision can help to communicate the importance of cultivating a culture of learning to all stakeholders. Also, the school vision will help to guide creation of goals that lead to the development of this culture. A school vision that includes this focus will ensure that school goals are aligned with a culture of learning and will help to establish and maintain the culture. When the school vision clearly incorporates a culture of learning, it will be apparent to all stakeholders that this is a key part of the school's purpose and focus.

School Goals

School goals help to determine where to devote energy and resources. When leaders set goals, they identify the necessary resources for achieving them. Goals must be aligned with the characteristics and outcomes of a culture of learning to ensure that the available resources, such as staff, funds, and time, are used to develop and maintain this culture. Rather than diverting resources to various competing goals, this will maximize the use of resources and effort. When a leader uses school goals to support a culture of learning, the culture will be strengthened as school goals are attained. The various aspects of a culture of learning can be incorporated into the school goals. For example, school goals can include high expectations for academic performance, goals related to college and career readiness for students, and implementation of student-centered instructional strategies for teachers.

Ensuring That School Goals Are Student-Centered

A leader can employee several strategies to ensure that school goals are student-centered. First, goals should be designed with student outcomes as a focus. These can include any outcome that is measured in terms of student-related data, such as academic performance or attendance. For example, a school leader may develop a school goal of increasing the campus attendance rate to 99% for the school year. This goal is directly related to a student outcome and the strategies that would be implemented to achieve this goal would directly benefit students. Second, all school goals should directly impact students. When developing goals, it is appropriate to ask how accomplishing the goal would impact students, as well as how students would be affected if the goal were not accomplished. If there is no impact to students, the goal is likely not student-centered. Third, goals should be developed with the purpose of benefitting all students. Student-centered goals do not marginalize or omit groups of students but benefit all students. For example, a school leader might set a school goal to increase test performance in reading for all students, not just those who have demonstrated deficiencies in prior performance.

Purpose of a School Vision

The purpose of a school vision is to convey the direction of the school to all stakeholders. A vision is a message or statement that describes how a leader envisions the school in the future. Through the school vision, the school's focus and priorities can be conveyed to all stakeholders, including staff, students, and the community. The school vision should inspire and motivate teachers and staff to pursue the school's goals. The school vision also provides direction for the teachers and staff in decision-making processes. All strategic planning should be guided by the school vision so that all goals and plans are designed with the purpose of achieving this vision. An example of a school vision is as follows: Our vision at XYZ Middle School is to equip and prepare students to be college and career ready, life-long learners, and responsible global citizens who are exemplary examples of the core values of respect, integrity, and perseverance.

Identifying Vision and Goals Based on Data and Research

<u>Types of Data Used to Develop a School Vision</u>

The majority of data that an education leader will have access to and be expected to analyze is quantitative data. This includes student academic performance data, attendance data, demographics, and many other key data points. Quantitative data can be analyzed using mathematical processes and can be represented in numerical form. For example, a school leader may calculate that the campus attendance rate is 96.8% annually or that 1 out of every 10 students receives special education services. Quantitative data can provide answers to "what" or "who" questions, but it cannot provide answers regarding "why" or "how." To understand why the data appears as it does, it is important for leaders to gather qualitative data from students, staff, and stakeholders. Qualitative data reflects opinions, perceptions, feelings, and assumptions. For example, a school leader may receive student concern about bullying on campus, or parents and community members may communicate to the school leader that the staff do not seem friendly. Quantitative and qualitative data should be used together to develop the vision for the school.

Sources of Data Used to Develop a School Vision

There are many sources of quantitative and qualitative data that a leader can use to develop a school vision. Sources of quantitative data include student academic performance data, attendance data, demographics, and other key data points. Student academic performance data is frequently used in developing a vision. Leaders can obtain this data from historical standardized test performance data, beginning-of-the year assessments in a variety of academic areas, teacher-assigned grades for classroom performance, and benchmark assessments. Qualitative data can be obtained from observations of teachers and students, feedback from teachers and students, focus groups, anonymous surveys, and other information from stakeholders. This type of information tells the education leader about school culture, values, attitudes, and beliefs. It should be used as a frame for understanding the quantitative data in order to gain a complete picture of the school's status.

Aligning School Goals with School Vision

The school vision describes how the leadership envisions the school in the future, and the school goals are the ways that the school will accomplish that vision. Each school goal should clearly demonstrate that by accomplishing the goal, the campus will be closer to realizing its vision. For example, a school may state in its vision that it will be a premier STEM (Science, Technology, Engineering, and Math) school. School leaders should work toward that vision by setting ambitious goals in the areas of science, technology, engineering, and math. Aligned goals could include the academic performance of students in these subject areas, increasing STEM course offerings, recruiting students for the STEM program, or earning awards and recognition in STEM competitions. An unaligned goal could be expanding the fine arts program. Aligning school goals with the school vision will ensure that all resources and energies are devoted to realizing the vision.

Using Data from Multiple Sources

It is important to use data from multiple sources to develop the school vision and goals because one source may portray a limited or skewed picture of the school. Using multiple sources can confirm the validity of data and provide a more complete picture of the complex dynamics of a school campus. For example, a school leader may obtain past academic data showing that fifth grade students have consistently performed at an advanced level. However, additional data may demonstrate that these students were already performing at an advanced level prior to fifth grade and were not growing academically. Additionally, using multiple sources of data can help a leader identify specific areas for improvement so that goals are targeted. For example, a leader of a high school may find that incoming ninth-grade students are consistently performing below standard in math. However, investigating which middle schools these students attended may reveal that the struggling students all attended the same middle school. Instead of assuming that math was an area of deficit for the ninth-grade class, this additional data could lead to a more specific goal in which resources are targeted.

Involving Stakeholders in Developing Vision

Stakeholders to Be Included

Stakeholders include anyone who has an interest in or is vested in the school. The primary stakeholders in schools are the children because they are most directly impacted by the decisions made regarding the school, so they should be engaged in the development of the school vision. Another significant group of stakeholders includes the school's faculty and staff because they are also directly impacted by the decisions. Other stakeholders include parents, district personnel, school board members, community members, and community business partners. A leader can involve these stakeholders in the development of the school vision by soliciting their opinions and feedback. This can be done through one-on-one interviews, focus groups, and community meetings, among other methods, to obtain their perspectives. Stakeholders can be motivated to engage in the development of the school vision when the school leader communicates a desire for their involvement and demonstrates respect for their input and opinions. This requires the school leader to devote time and opportunity to meet with various stakeholders and to engage in conversation regarding the school vision.

It is important to involve stakeholders in the development of the school vision to incorporate a variety of perspectives and to increase buy-in for the vision. Often, school leaders who are in the process of developing a vision for the school are new to the position, so they cannot be expected to know every aspect of the school dynamics or all the nuances of the campus. It is important to involve stakeholders in the process of developing the vision so that the leader can have as much information as possible. Also, including stakeholders in the process creates buy-in. If stakeholders believe that their feelings and opinions have been disregarded in the creation of the vision, it can lead to disengagement in the goals aligned to that vision or even to opposition. A leader wants all stakeholders to be advocates of the school vision, so stakeholders must be included in the development of the school vision.

Reaching Consensus Among Stakeholders

When engaging stakeholders in the development of the school vision and goals, it can be a challenge to reach consensus, especially when viewpoints seem to conflict. It is important for a school leader to clearly communicate how consensus will be fairly achieved. Stakeholders who are aware of the process for providing input before participating will know what to expect and are more likely to be receptive to compromise in the event of dissension. Additionally, the leader must be respectful of all input and must acknowledge opinions and perspectives, even if they are not aligned with his or her own or the majority. Incorporating voting processes, such as an anonymous ballot or online survey, can facilitate the use of the majority's viewpoints without identifying dissenters. Finally, the school leader must convey that, although the stakeholders' input is valued and will be considered, he or she still retains the ultimate responsibility for decision making.

Meeting Diverse Needs

Address Equity Issues Related to Race, Diversity, and Access

When developing the school vision and goals, a school leader must ensure that all students—regardless of race, religion, academic background, or education access—will be successful. When collecting data to inform the development of the school vision and goals, a school leader should determine whether any groups of students have been disenfranchised in the past and, if so, how the school vision and goals can be designed to prevent that disenfranchisement from happening in the future. For example, a school leader may find that historically students who are of limited English proficiency (LEP) have not performed as well as their peers in math on standardized tests. This may necessitate the design of additional goals to support the improvement of LEP students in math. Equity does not mean equality. Equity means that some groups of students may need additional resources and support in order for them to meet performance standards. The school vision and goals must take into account the strengths and needs of all students so that all can receive an equitable education and be successful.

Identifying the Diverse Needs of Students

Students have diverse needs and not all of these needs can be predicted based on the students' demographic groups. For example, not all students in poverty have the same needs, nor do all students who speak limited English. The school leader should make an effort to identify student needs so they can be addressed in the development of the school's vision and goals. A leader can identify these needs by speaking directly to students. This gives students the opportunity to articulate their own needs. Also, the leader can speak with families to identify additional student needs. This is particularly helpful when students are young and cannot accurately identify their own needs. Finally, the school leader can observe students in the school and identify deficit areas of the school program. For example, the school leader may notice that many students arrive late to school and are tired and hungry when they arrive. The school leader can then use observation data to inform the development of the school goals and vision.

Plan for Implementing the Vision and Goals

Importance of Developing an Implementation Plan

To achieve a school vision and goals, a plan must be in place. A well-constructed plan serves as a guide for how the goals will be accomplished. Having a plan conveys to stakeholders that the vision and goals are feasible and instills confidence in the campus administration. A plan also serves as a framework for directing the actions of a leadership team and campus faculty and staff. Additionally, a leader cannot be everywhere all the time, so having a plan in place ensures that progress can be made, even in the leader's absence. Finally, having a plan helps to keep the efforts of leadership and staff focused. Many aspects of a school campus can become distractions to the primary goals and these distractions can cause leaders to divert resources and efforts to the wrong areas. A plan keeps efforts and resources focused and purposeful, which increases the plan's chance of being effective.

Components of an Effective Plan

An effective plan should include action steps, persons responsible, time frames, milestones, resources needed, and evidence of implementation. The action steps in a plan should clearly outline what needs to be done to accomplish the plan. These steps should be broken down so that someone who did not participate in developing the plan can understand what needs to be done. An effective plan also identifies the persons responsible for each aspect of the plan. If no one is held accountable for the actions to accomplish the plan, they likely will not get done. The plan should also be time bound. This will help to identify whether the plan is on track for completion. Milestones serve as checkpoints that also help to determine the progress of the plan. The plan will include the resources needed to accomplish it so that these resources are planned for and obtained. This will prevent delay in accomplishing the plan. Finally, the evidence of implementation should be included in the plan so that ongoing monitoring can take place. Evidence of implementation could include documents, visible indicators, or regular meetings, depending on the aspect of the plan.

Barriers to Implementing the Vision and Goals Effectively

Both expected and unexpected barriers may arise when implementing the vision and goals. It can be expected that stakeholders who did not wholeheartedly agree with the creation of the vision and goals may be reluctant to implement the plan to achieve them. This can be a barrier because a lack of support for or direct opposition to the vision and goals can delay progress. Many unexpected barriers may also arise. These may include changes in district policy and procedure, changes in state law, shortfalls in school budgets, and staff changes, among others. For example, standardized test performance expectations or adoption of a new test can affect goals. Additionally, the loss of a teacher or the promotion of a leadership team member could also affect the successful implementation of the vision and goals. Some school districts have experienced unexpected loss of instructional time due to inclement weather conditions, creating a barrier to accomplishing school goals.

Identifying barriers

When planning the implementation of the school vision and goals, the school leader may encounter barriers that will slow the planning process. One barrier is attempting to analyze too much data. Data is valuable to the planning process, but an abundance of data can become overwhelming and delay progress. The school leader must identify what data is needed and what can be put aside. Another barrier is the lack of consensus from other stakeholders who are providing input to the development of the plan. Stakeholders such as community members, parents, and staff may have conflicting ideas and suggestions related to the development of the vision and goals. The leader must determine which feedback to incorporate in the plan, as not all ideas are sound or can be prioritized. Finally, a barrier that can be difficult to overcome is garnering support for the implementation of change on campus. In most instances, a school leader will be appointed in the place of a predecessor who already had a school vision and goals in place. Stakeholders may be resistant to drastic changes in the school vision and goals, so the school leader must overcome these objections to do what is best for the students.

Overcoming Potential Barriers

A leader can employee various strategies to overcome potential barriers to implementing the vision and goals effectively. To overcome lack of support of the vision and goals, the leader can include as many stakeholders as possible in the development of the vision and goals. This will increase buy-in and communicate the vision and goals often so that stakeholders are reminded of the school's focus. A leader can also include strategies in the action plan to address potential barriers, such as loss of staff. For example, a leader can designate teams, rather than individuals, to work on components of the plan. Therefore, if a staff member is lost, other team members can continue implementation of a goal. The leader can also consider actions or contingency plans to enact if barriers arise. For example, if a goal requires a designated number of new computers, a leader may consider what to do if a budget shortfall allows for the purchase of only half of the computers.

Supporting the Implementation by Leading by Example

Leading by example can support the implementation of the school vision and goals by inspiring others, conveying priorities, and garnering support from stakeholders. When a leader sets an example of expected behavior, staff and students will be inspired to participate and to follow the leader's example, implementing the vision and goals in the same way as their leader. This increases the effort devoted to accomplishing the vision and goals. When the leader engages in behaviors that implement the vision and goals, this conveys to stakeholders that the vision and goals are priorities because this is where the leader chooses to devote time. When a leader's priorities are clear to stakeholders, it is easier for the leader to encourage them to participate in those prioritized activities and to implement action plans related to those priorities. For example, if a leader makes it evident through his or her own actions that reading instruction is a priority for the campus, then stakeholders will expect and support further initiatives relating to reading instruction. In contrast, when a leader's actions do not match the goals and vision, this results in a mixed message to stakeholders.

Aligning Human, Fiscal, and Material Resources

The strategies and initiatives for implementing the vision and goals require resources, so a leader must ensure that all human, fiscal, and material resources are aligned to the vision and goals. Aligning resources to the vision and goals will ensure fewer barriers to implementation. In contrast, when resources are not aligned to the vision and goals, not only will leaders find it difficult to implement the mission and vision, they will also find that their efforts are diverted to the other areas that the resources have been devoted to. This results in a less significant impact of those resources for the benefit of students and the campus as a whole. For example, if the vision for the school is to have state-of-the-art technology for classroom instruction, the leader must ensure that there are qualified staff members who are able to utilize the technology, funds for the purchase of technology hardware and software, and additional resources such as storage and server space for the additional technology. If any aspect of the resources is misaligned, there is a possibility that the goal or vision will not be obtained.

Delegating

A leader cannot do an effective job without support. In order to balance the duties and responsibilities of being a campus leader, an effective leader must identify tasks and activities that can be delegated to other leadership team members or administrative staff. If a leader does not delegate tasks and responsibilities, he or she may be overwhelmed and unable to meet all of the demands necessary to implement the mission and vision. When a leader designs an action plan for accomplishing the vision and goals, he or she must also identify the staff members who can complete those actions. For example, another member of the leadership team can be assigned a specific project, such as hosting the quarterly community literacy nights for the school year. Also, a clerical staff person can assist the leader in designing and formatting documents related to a project. The role of the leader is to lead and manage a team that can implement the vision, not to implement the vision independently and individually. Delegation is also important when the leader is not on campus or available. This ensures that the work of accomplishing the vision and goals will continue even in the leader's absence.

Measurable Expectations

Using Data to Support Measurable Expectations

Data can support the setting and tracking of measurable expectations. When a leader uses data to communicate expectations to faculty and staff, it increases the staff's ability to meet those expectations and helps staff to determine if they are meeting expectations. For example, a leader can set the expectation that teachers and staff maintain a 98% attendance rate at work. Setting this measurable expectation makes it easier for staff to self-regulate and also helps leaders to address failure to meet expectations. By using data, a leader can determine if expectations are being met, which can help determine whether the school is on track to meet or exceed goals. For example, a leader may expect 90% of students to meet performance standards in reading. If 93% of students meet performance standards, the leader will know that the expectation is being exceeded and it is likely that the school will meet their goal. In contrast, when data is not used to support expectations, it can be difficult to determine progress toward meeting expectations, identify potential areas of weakness, or address failures to meet expectations.

Using Measurable Expectations to Identify Trends and Patterns

The identification of trends and patterns in school performance can be valuable in forming action plans so that decision-making can be targeted and strategic. When expectations are measurable, the data that is collected and analyzed can reveal patterns and trends. For example, if a leader were to review student reading progress, using data from the last three assessments, it may be revealed that a particular demographic group is consistently underperforming. This trend can help the leader provide targeted resources and interventions to meet the reading performance expectation. Similarly, an analysis of student attendance data may reveal a pattern of poor attendance on rainy days. Identifying this pattern can help the leader to address the barriers that rainy days create for student attendance so that students can meet attendance expectations.

Monitoring Progress Toward Goals

A leader must monitor progress toward goals to increase the likelihood of meeting those goals. Leaders should check the progress of goals in regular intervals throughout the school year based on these measurable expectations. This allows the leader to determine if the school is on track to meet a goal and, if not, allows time to make changes to the action plan. For example, a leader may set an annual goal for 90% of students to meet academic performance expectations in math on standardized tests. This goal could be broken down into measurable expectations, such as performance on particular math standards, which are reviewed at regular intervals, like every three weeks. If a leader were to determine that at least 90% of students were not successful on a particular math standard, this could indicate a danger of not meeting the annual goal. However, because this data was obtained before the administration of the standardized test, the leader has time to develop and implement interventions such as math tutorials, increasing the likelihood of meeting the goal.

Supporting High Expectations with Measurable Expectations

Measurable expectations support high expectations because they clearly define the expectations for students and staff, as well as the standard used to measure the expectation. A measurable expectation can lead to higher expectations of performance because it is clear and facilitates monitoring. When expectations are not measurable, the result is ambiguity or confusion. It can be difficult for a person to know if he or she is meeting expectations and this ambiguity can convey that they will not be monitored. In contrast, when expectations are measurable, a leader can clearly convey how students and staff can meet those expectations and how they will be monitored. For example, if a leader sets a general expectation for high student performance in math, teachers may be confused about the performance indicators and subsequently have varying expectations for math performance and how students can demonstrate that performance, such as classwork, homework, and exams. In contrast, a leader could set an expectation that all students will maintain a passing grade in math classes and pass all math exams. The leader can then monitor the expectation by reviewing class and exam grades so that those who are not meeting expectations can be addressed.

Discriminating Between Vision and Goals That Are Measurable and Non-Measurable for All Students

Measurable vs. Non-Measurable Goals

Measurable goals can be quantified and non-measurable goals cannot be quantified. An example of a measurable goal is: 95% of 8th grade students will earn a score of 70% or above on the math benchmark exam. This goal is measurable because it can be determined whether or not it was met by calculating the percentage of students who demonstrated the defined proficiency on the exam. It also identifies what performance is expected of the students in order to reach the goal. When goals are measurable, it is easy to determine whether or not they have been met. In contrast, a non-measurable goal may be ambiguous and it may be difficult to determine whether or not it has been met. An example of a non-measurable goal is: 8th grade students will be successful on the math benchmark exam. This goal is not measurable because it does not state how students demonstrate success on the benchmark exam, nor how many students must be successful to meet the goal.

Converting Non-Measurable Goals into Measurable Goals

Non-measurable goals can be converted into measurable goals by making them quantifiable. To make goals quantifiable, the leader must determine how success is measured for each behavior identified in the goal and how to know that success has been achieved. When a goal involves a performance standard or assessment, it should be clearly identified. For example, rather than using the phrase "demonstrate proficiency" in a goal, the leader should identify what constitutes proficiency, such as earning a particular score. Some goals involve behaviors that are not easily quantifiable, such as goals related to culture or attitudes. In these instances, a leader must determine how these behaviors will be measured, such as by observations or surveys. For example, a leader may wish all staff to be perceived as courteous. The leader can survey students and parents regarding the courtesy of staff and set a goal of an average rating of 4 out of 5 or greater in the area of courtesy. Alternatively, the leader may use observations to measure the goal, such as requiring front office personal to greet all visitors immediately upon entry 100% of the time.

Ineffectiveness of Non-Measurable Goals

Non-measurable goals can often be ineffective because they do not clearly convey how to achieve the goal or how one knows when the goal has been achieved. When there is no measure of what constitutes success, then those working toward the goal will identify their own perception of success, which may not be in line with the leader's expectations. For example, if the goal is for all 5th grade students to be successful on a test, a leader may expect students to earn scores of 90% or greater and the teacher may expect scores of 70% or greater. In order to ensure clarity of goals and to help develop strategies to reach those goals, the goals must be measurable. This ensures that all know the exact target that they are trying to reach and can determine if and when they have reached the target.

Understanding Laws at Various Levels

Relationship Between Federal, State, and Local Educational Laws, Policies, and Practices

Almost all aspects of the education process are governed by laws, policies, and practices. Laws governing the education process are established at the national and state level and supersede district and campus policies. Federal laws take precedence over state laws. State laws supplement and complement the federal laws. Local education agencies (LEAs) then interpret federal and state laws to create policies for their school districts that help schools to adhere to those laws or to clarify areas that the laws do not explicitly address. Individual campuses create procedures to address areas not explicitly outlined by district policy. For example, federal law states that students must be assessed by a standardized exam for grade promotion and graduation. State law dictates which tests the students take and when they are tested. School districts determine the policies for administering those tests, within the guidelines set by the state. Campuses implement district policy and may incorporate their own practices such as cell phone policies, dress code polices, or other school day aspects that are impacted by testing. Whenever there is a conflict between law and policy, law takes precedence.

Areas of the Education Process Impacted by Laws

Federal and state laws impact almost every aspect of the education process. Often these laws require additional policies and procedures to ensure adherence to the laws. However, there are specific areas of the education process that are highly impacted by federal and state law. These include educating students with disabilities, educating English language learners, standardized testing, student confidentiality, school liability, school performance expectations, technology use, school finance, and many more. School leaders must understand the laws and how these laws can influence the development and implementation of their vision and goals. While many school districts develop policies and practices that aid school leaders in adhering to the law, it is the school leader's responsibility to remain current on school law at both the state and federal levels.

Impact of Laws and Policies on Professional Ethics

Federal and state laws dictate the requirements that educators must meet to be certified. As part of these requirements, educators must adhere to ethical codes and standards of behavior. The ethical codes address areas such as general conduct, conduct toward colleagues, and conduct toward students. Educators are expected to adhere to these standards of behavior; otherwise, sanctions may be placed on their educator licenses or their licenses and certifications may even be revoked. On any given school day, an education leader may make a number of decisions and must be fully aware of the legal and ethical ramifications of each one. Additionally, school leaders must understand that ethical decision-making is not only a result of personal morals and values but also of codes and standards of behavior that are set forth by federal and state government. The code of ethics requires that educators abide by all laws, but some decisions address "gray areas" in which there are no explicit laws, policies, or procedures. In these instances, school leaders must ensure that their decisions align with the educator code of ethics.

Development of Policies

Schools and school districts often develop policies as a safeguard for staff and students. Laws enacted at the federal and/or state level are often broad and subject to interpretation. As a result, policies are developed to define specific actions and behaviors that adhere to those laws, with the purpose of trying to ensure that persons abide by the law by adhering to policies. Policies are meant to be a protection to those who adhere to them. For example, a law may broadly state that schools must administer a confidentially secure assessment of student performance in Math and Reading. The school district may then develop policies to ensure that tests are administered to students in a confidential and secure manner. A person who violates a policy does not necessarily violate a law, but this is possible. School leaders and school staff should abide by local policies as a protection, ensuring that they are adhering to state and federal laws.

Relationship Between Vision and Goals with Legal Responsibilities

Aligning Vision and Goals to School, Local, State, and Federal Policies

The school vision and goals must be aligned to school, local, state, and federal policies so that they can be legally and ethically accomplished. If the school vision and goals are not aligned to these laws and policies, it is possible that working toward these goals would constitute breaking the law or violating policy. Because laws and policies supersede campus initiatives, it is important to align goals to these so that resources can be used efficiently. Even if the misalignment of the goal to the laws and policies does not constitute a violation of the law or policy, it could cause resources and efforts to be diverted, resulting in loss of efficiency and impact. For example, students with disabilities may require additional academic services, as dictated in special education law and policy. The campus leader must provide the resources necessary to meet these students' needs, so it would be efficient to align the school's other goals and resources to this requirement.

Communicating School Laws and Policies to the Community

It is important to communicate school laws and policies to the community so that they can be informed of the requirements and constraints that govern the school leader's actions, decision-making, and goal-setting. The community should be aware of the laws and policies that helped to shape the school leader's vision for the school. The community may be unaware of laws and policies that can influence the operations of the school and how these laws and policies may affect the feasibility of their ideas and suggestions. For example, the community may wish to do away with a particular extracurricular sport because of low participation and lack of performance by the athletes, but they may be unaware that certain sports must be offered on campus due to compliance to Title IX of education law. A principal could explain that the current education law requires that the particular sport be offered so that there is no perceived discrimination in sport offerings at the school.

Impact of Laws, Regulations, Policies, and Procedures on Development and Implementation of Vision and Goals

Laws, regulations, policies, and procedures should be reviewed and considered during the development and implementation of campus vision and goals. Adherence to these laws and regulations supersede campus initiatives, so it is efficient and effective to align these with the vision and goals to prevent conflict or inefficiency in use of resources. A leader can evaluate these first, and then determine how the vision and goals can be designed in a way to help the school meet or exceed these regulations. For example, if accountability standards require that schools have a passing rate of 90% or above for the state exam in reading, then the school leader should set a goal to meet or exceed that requirement. If the school leader were to set the school goal at 85%, then meeting the school goal would still cause the school to fail according to state accountability standards. In order to be strategic, a school leader should determine what is expected of the school according to law and policy, and then determine how their vision and goals can align with those laws and policies.

Clear Communication

Importance of the Clear Communication of the Vision and Goals

It is important to communicate the campus vision and goals clearly so that stakeholders can understand and support them. If the vision and goals are unclear, stakeholders may have difficulty determining if they support the vision and goals or what to expect on the campus when the vision and goals are implemented. To communicate clearly, a leader should avoid technical terms and jargon that may not be easily understood by stakeholders. For example, a leader can communicate to stakeholders that the campus goal is to increase reading performance, rather than referring to a specific reading program or strategy that may not be familiar to them. Clear communication of campus vision and goals helps to garner support from stakeholders for campus initiatives. When communication is clear, the vision and goals can be easily aligned with outside support and resources from the district, community, and state and federal programs.

Determining If Communication of Vision and Goals to Stakeholders Is Clear and Effective

A leader will know if the communication of vision and goals to stakeholders is clear and effective by observing the stakeholders' behavior. When the vision and goals are clear, stakeholders are more likely to buy in to the leader's vision and assist in achieving it. Stakeholders who understand the vision and goals can articulate them in their own words. They will be able to communicate the vision and goals to other stakeholders and to the leader. Their behavior will be aligned to the vision and goals as well. Also, stakeholders who understand the vision will propose ideas and actions that are aligned to the vision, avoiding those that are opposed or a distraction to the vision. When the communication of the vision and goals is clear and effective, all stakeholders will understand the vision and goals and how they can participate in achieving them.

Hierarchical Communication

Hierarchical communication refers to communicating up and down the chain of command. Leaders communicate up by communicating with superiors, such as district office staff or the superintendent. Leaders communicate down by communicating with faculty and staff. Communicating with various members of the hierarchy often takes different communication skills. For example, communicating with a supervisor may involve responding to specific requests or demands or demonstrating alignment of campus vision and goals with the school district's vision and initiatives. Communicating up may occur via emails and memorandums, meetings, or visits on campus. In contrast, communicating with faculty and staff requires communicating in a way that inspires them to perform as a team in order to achieve the campus vision and goals. This type of communication also involves holding campus team members accountable for their performance. This communication may occur via emails or memorandums, faculty meetings, or in professional learning communities. Leaders must recognize their audience when communicating so that they can use the most effective communication strategy.

Communicating Implementation of the Vision and Goals

A leader must ensure that stakeholders are aware of how the various campus initiatives and actions align to the school vision and goals. A leader can do this by frequently and clearly identifying this alignment. This can be communicated in writing or verbally. Campus plans for the implementation of the vision and goals should identify the planned initiatives and activities. For example, if the school's vision is to achieve excellence in literacy, the leader could indicate in the campus plan that the school will host a literacy night. At the literacy night, the leader should clearly explain to participants that it is a strategy for achieving the goal of excellence in literacy. The leader could also include the school's vision statement on the agenda for the literacy night. A leader cannot assume that all stakeholders understand the connection between the day-to-day campus activities and the vision and goals. Therefore, the leader needs to verbally explain the connection between campus activities or initiatives and the vision at every opportunity.

Communicating the Vision and Goals Through Others

A school leader can utilize other persons to help communicate the vision and goals. Members of the leadership team can help. Often, these other school leaders come into contact with staff and parents more frequently than the principal and therefore have more opportunities to convey the vision and goals. Additionally, parents can be instrumental. Parent leaders, such as those who lead parent organizations or are influential in the community, can help to spread the word about the school vision and goals. Also, in diverse communities, staff members who speak multiple languages may be utilized to communicate the school vision and goals to parents and communities members of a variety of backgrounds. When stakeholders hear the vision and goals from persons other than the leader, they will perceive that the vision and goals are supported and are more likely to support them as well. In order for this type of communication to be effective, the school leader must ensure that all have a sound understanding of the school vision and goals before sharing them with others.

Communicating to Staff, Families, and Students

Communicating the Campus Vision and Goals to Stakeholders

Leaders can clearly communicate the campus vision and goals to stakeholders using verbal, written, and nonverbal communication. Leaders can communicate verbally by formally hosting meetings and events that help to share the vision and goals for the campus. Leaders can host community meetings and invite parents, community members, and other stakeholders to attend. These meetings are opportunities for the leader to clarify and elaborate on the vision and goals. Leaders can also hold staff meetings and student assemblies with those on campus. Additionally, the vision and goals should be verbalized at every opportunity. A leader can use written communication to communicate the vision and goals, such as in formal reports, emails, and memorandums. For example, some leaders incorporate the school's vision in the footer of formal written documents so that it is always visible. All written communication should align to the vision and reinforce the goals for the campus. Finally, the leader's behavior can serve as a nonverbal communication of the vision and goals. For example, if the vision of the school is to cultivate students who are life-long learners, then the leader can model this behavior by reading, participating in training, and taking classes.

Timely Communication to Staff, Families, and Students

Timely communication requires proper planning. The calendar of events for the school year should be outlined in advance. The leader needs to identify the types of communication to share at various periods throughout the year, such as the beginning of the school year, school holidays, testing periods, and others. A leader must also provide advance notice so that staff and families can properly prepare and plan for school events and activities. Leaders can provide this advance notice using calendars, announcements, flyers, and phone calls. Communicating in multiple ways ensures that the communication is received in a timely manner. There can be an abundance of information about events, activities, and other aspects of the school that needs to be shared with staff, families, and students, so the leader should delegate the aggregation and dissemination of this information to other staff as necessary. The leader can set expectations for how these staff members communicate to families and students. For example, if a school department hosts an event, the event should be placed on the school calendar and parents should be informed with sufficient time to prepare for and support the event.

Two-Way Process of Effective Communication

The act of communication involves a sender and a receiver. If communication is sent but not received, it is not effective. A leader can increase the possibility of effective communication by using a variety of mediums. These may include phone calls, meetings, emails, memorandums, and formal letters or documents. Additionally, a leader can survey stakeholders to determine the preferred mode of communication. For communication to be deemed effective, leaders must confirm that it has been received. Leaders can request a response or feedback on the communication so that it is acknowledged and the leader can be sure that the message was received in the intended way. Effective communication also means that the leader can be the receiver of communication, not just the sender. Leaders should be open to taking phone calls, responding to emails, or participating in meetings that allow others to communicate with them. When the leader acts as the receiver, he or she should acknowledge that the message was received so the sender is aware that the communication was effective.

Steps to Take When Miscommunication Occurs

If the leader becomes aware of a miscommunication, he or she should act immediately to correct it. Failing to correct a miscommunication can lead to confusion, conflict, and lack of engagement in and support of the school program. First, the leader should identify the miscommunication. Then the leader should make an effort to correct it by acknowledging that the message was not sent properly and providing the correct message. For example, a school leader could notify parents that the school's art program would not be part of the vision for the upcoming school year, and the parents might infer that the art program would be eliminated. The school leader should inform parents that the art program will not be eliminated and then explain how it would be affected in the upcoming school year. The school leader should also assume responsibility for the initial ineffective communication.

Culture of Learning

Evidence of a Leader's Vision and Goals

It is the leader's goal to develop a culture of learning on campus. The leader must incorporate this goal into the school vision and goals. As a result, when there is evidence of a culture of learning on campus, this is also evidence that the leader's vision and goals are being implemented. In a culture of learning, both adults and students work toward learning goals and are self-motivated to achieve these goals. They also have access to the necessary resources to support and drive engagement in the learning process. Evidence of the culture of learning includes students and staff who are goal-oriented and self-motivated to learn and engage in the learning process, motivation to perform at the highest levels academically, and skilled use of available resources to engage in the learning process. When these are present, it will be evident that the vision and goals can be accomplished.

Support a Culture of Learning by Communicating the Vision and Goals to Stakeholders

When the vision and goals are communicated effectively to stakeholders, they can in turn support the culture of learning. When stakeholders know and understand the vision, they can identify how to support it and help to develop the culture of learning. For example, if a business stakeholder in the community becomes aware of the school's vision to implement technology in the classroom to develop a culture of learning, he or she may decide to donate computers for a computer lab. Had the stakeholder not known that the school could benefit from the donation, he or she may not have taken that action. All stakeholders may not be in a position to give to the school, but they can support the culture of learning through their participation in school and community events and by advocating for the school and its needs to school and government representatives. Communicating the vision and goals to stakeholders increases the number of people who can offer their support in implementation.

Instructional Leadership

Commitment to High Standards for All Students

Equity vs. Equality

All students are expected to meet the standards outlined by the state and federal governments. School leaders are responsible for providing students with the instruction, resources, and support necessary to meet these standards. Equality refers to providing all students with the same amount of resources and support, regardless of their needs. Equity refers to providing students with the resources and support that meet their individual needs. An example of equality would be that all students receive ninety minutes of reading instruction each day. An example of equity would be that students who have shown deficiencies in reading receive an extra thirty minutes of reading instruction each day. When leaders implement equity in schools, this may mean that some students receive more resources and support than others, or different support and resources. Leaders must be aware of what students need so that the right resources and support can be used to support these students. This need may be due to a lack of educational opportunity, physical or intellectual disabilities, or other circumstances. All students need resources and support to enrich their education, but practicing equity means that students will receive the appropriate amount of resources based on their identified needs.

Creating a Culture of High Expectations

A culture of high expectations means that staff and students strive toward high goals and excellence. A leader can create a culture of high expectations by setting campus goals above minimum standards. For example, if the required student attendance rate is 90%, the leader can set a goal for a 95% attendance rate for the campus. The leader can also reward student and staff performance that exceeds expectations. For example, the leader may publicly celebrate students who achieve Honor Roll. Another strategy for creating a culture of high expectations is to provide models of excellence for students and staff. These models can be effective programs on other campuses, role models in the community, or exemplary staff and students on campus. To create a culture of high expectations, a leader must also address performance that does not meet expectations in an effective manner. It must be clear to staff and students that performing below expectations is not acceptable. The leader must also provide the resources necessary for staff and students to meet the high expectations that have been set.

Evident on a School Campus

It is evident that a school has a culture of high expectations by what is seen and heard on campus. The culture of high expectations is evidenced by the campus appearance, including its cleanliness, organization, and posted materials. Bulletin boards and other visual aids in the hallways and in classrooms should demonstrate high expectations for academic achievement, character, and behavior. For example, a school may post college pennants and posters in the hallways to demonstrate an expectation that students are college-ready. Also, the instruction that is observed in the classroom should be evidence of high expectations for students and their ability to perform academically. The culture of high expectations is also evidenced by how students and staff speak. When there are high expectations, teachers and students speak positively about learning and meeting goals. There is little to no negative talk in regard to learning and performance. Instead there is problem-solving, brainstorming, and action-planning to meet academic goals. A culture of high expectations on campus is evidenced by the performance, which is indicated by goal attainment and student performance data.

Evident in the Classroom

Within the classroom, a culture of high expectations is evident by the appearance of the classroom and the behavior of teacher and students. First, the classroom will be neat, organized, and conducive to learning. Posted materials will be academically relevant, positive, and encouraging. In a classroom with a culture of high expectations, the teacher begins class on time and is prepared for the lesson. Materials and technology are ready for the start of class and there is a clear objective for the day's lesson. The teacher makes an effort to engage all students and uses a variety of instructional strategies to do so. In this classroom, students are eager to participate and remain engaged in the lesson throughout its entirety. Students demonstrate engagement in and mastery of the content by engaging in discussion with the teacher and their peers. There are few, if any, behavioral problems in this type of classroom, and if they do arise the teacher addresses them quickly and appropriately. There is evidence in the classroom of a good relationship and rapport between the teacher and the students and no students are allowed to disengage from the lesson.

Identify Achievement Gaps

Achievement Gap

The term "achievement gap" refers to the disparity in educational performance of students of low socioeconomic status, minority students, and female students. Educational performance is measured by many indicators such as course grades, pass/fail rates and promotion, standardized test performance, course selection, graduation rates, college enrollment rates, and many other indicators. The achievement gap exists as a national phenomenon but is also observed at the state level, district level, and even within campuses. The achievement gap was identified over fifty years ago and continues today. There is an abundance of research regarding why it exists and how to address it at all educational levels, but so far there has not been any success in eliminating it. As a result, leaders should be prepared to identify and address achievement gaps on their campuses.

Determining the Existence of an Achievement Gap on Campus

The best way to determine the existence of an achievement gap on campus is to analyze student performance indicators. Leaders can use a variety of performance indicators to identify if an achievement gap exists on their campus and, if so, for whom. Leaders can analyze performance data for standardized tests administered over the past 2–3 years to identify any disparities. The data should be compared based on socioeconomic status, race and ethnicity, gender, special education status, limited English proficiency status, and any other subgroups that are relevant to the campus. If an achievement gap exists, students in a particular subgroup will consistently perform at a lower rate when compared to the other groups of students. This method of analysis should be repeated for other performance indicators such as grades, pass/fail rates, promotion and retention, graduation, and any others that are relevant to the campus goals.

Determining the Existence of an Achievement Gap Outside of the Campus

A school leader may evaluate data on campus and determine that all students, regardless of demographics, are performing academically at comparable rates. This is often the case in schools with little to no diversity. However, a lack of evidence of an achievement gap within a campus does not mean that students are not affected by it. The school leader should compare the performance of students on his or her campus to other schools in the surrounding area, both within and outside of the school district. The leader may then find that his or her students are not performing at the same level as students in other schools. For example, a school leader may find that the majority of students on his or her campus are demonstrating a proficiency of 76% in math, while students in other schools are demonstrating a proficiency of 88%. Consequently, the school leader may realize that students at his or her school need to improve in math to remain on pace with their academic peers.

Planning to Reduce Gaps

Reducing the Achievement Gap

To reduce the achievement gap on campus, leaders should assess the needs of the underperforming groups of students and align resources and support in an equitable manner. Leaders can provide targeted interventions to these students based on their identified needs. For example, the leader may schedule math and reading tutorials for a particular subgroup of students who have demonstrated deficiencies in that area. A leader should also set campus goals that specifically address the performance of underperforming groups of students. This will ensure that there is an action plan for addressing the needs of these students, as well as specific resources dedicated to their performance. Finally, a leader should track data for the performance indicators that show the achievement gap. This data should be collected and analyzed at regular intervals so that additional interventions, resources, and support can be implemented, if necessary. In order to reduce the achievement gap, the leader should target these students with resources and support and monitor their progress on a regular basis.

Addressing the Achievement Gap

Goal-Setting

Goal-setting can help to address the achievement gap because it focuses attention on the groups of students who need extra support and helps to target resources in those areas. Areas in which school leaders create goals receive attention and targeted resources. When goals are developed that specifically address areas of the school programming with evidence of an achievement gap, the school leader can turn the focus of students, staff, and the community to these areas. Additionally, when goals are created, there is a determination to accomplish those goals, so if a goal is related to the achievement gap, it is more likely that the gap will be addressed. For example, if the school leader has seen evidence in the data that Hispanic students with limited English proficiency are lagging behind their peers in reading performance, the school leader can develop a school goal that specifically addresses the reading performance of Hispanic students with limited English proficiency. As a result, there would be increased focus on all Hispanic students with limited English proficiency, including the dedication of time, effort, and resources.

Data Monitoring

Data monitoring can be used to address the achievement gap because it can help to identify areas of the school program where the gap exists and to monitor changes in the achievement gap on campus. First, data should be used to identify where an achievement gap is present. The achievement gap is typically present in reading and math content areas, but can vary among other subject areas, as well as by groups of students. For example, a school leader may find that there is a gap in math performance between African American students and their peers, but that the gap is largest among African American males. Additionally, the data can show the school leader where the gap may be narrowing due to the instructional strategies and changes in school programming, or where the gap has shifted to another group of students. Therefore, data monitoring is key in identifying the achievement gap, determining the efficacy of strategies implemented to address the achievement gap, and assessing changes in the achievement gap among other student populations.

Rigor and Relevance

Rigor

Rigor in academic instruction refers to challenging curriculum and instruction. Rigorous instruction challenges students not only academically, but also intellectually, and even personally. Rigorous instruction is often complex and challenges students to think deeply and critically. Through rigorous instruction, students are able to develop the soft skills necessary for success in college, career, and adulthood, such as problem-solving, critical thinking, inferring, studying, time management, self-discipline, working in teams, and many others. Rigor does not mean something is excessively hard or difficult. However, rigor does involve stimulating, engaging instruction. Rigorous instruction often requires students to make connections across academic content areas and apply concepts to the real world. For example, if a high school English teacher wanted to assign a rigorous assignment based on a reading of *To Kill a Mockingbird*, he or she could assign a project in which students discuss the impact of the political setting in the United States at the time of the story on the plot. In contrast, a non-rigorous assignment could be a worksheet of multiple-choice questions.

Ensuring Rigor in the Instructional Program

A school leader must ensure that all students have access to a rigorous instructional program. First, a leader must evaluate the curriculum for alignment to state standards. This ensures that all curriculum is designed to instruct students based on the expectations set by the state. This prevents the lowering of standards in the classroom, which could lead to students falling behind. Next, a leader must determine that curriculum is taught in a rigorous manner. This includes creating lessons that require students to think critically. A leader may encourage instructional strategies such as differentiated instruction, project-based learning, and collaborative learning to help foster rigorous instruction in the classroom. Finally, the school leader must ensure that assessment of instruction is rigorous. This may mean encouraging the use of projects and other creative means that allow students to demonstrate mastery of standards and objectives. A rigorous instructional program avoids reliance on worksheets and other assessment activities that do not align with a rigorous instructional program.

How Campus Goals Can Support Rigorous Instruction

Rigorous instruction is challenging yet feasible for students. Campus goals can support rigorous instruction by motivating instructional staff to have high expectations for teaching and learning. When a goal is set high, it challenges instructional staff to work harder and with greater urgency, which requires utilizing rigorous instruction. For example, if a campus has had prior reading performance of 65%, a campus goal of 70% would not require significant change from the prior year's strategies and practice. However, setting a reading performance goal of 80% for the school year would encourage teachers to provide rigorous instruction to students to meet the higher performance expectation. Low expectations in goal setting will result in low expectations in instruction and high expectations in goal setting will result in high expectations in instruction. Similarly, when campus goals include all populations and sub-populations of students, rigorous instruction is supported. This ensures that low-performing students and high-performing students receive instruction at their appropriate level of rigor.

Benefits of Cross-Curricular Instruction

Cross-curricular instruction is the deliberate making of connections between various content areas so that students may apply their knowledge in more than one content area at a time. For example, students may examine the historical setting of a story in a reading class, utilize math strategies in a science class, or discuss geometric principles in an art class. Cross-curricular instruction is beneficial for students because it demonstrates the relevance of their content knowledge. When students understand that the instruction is not isolated to one particular area, but has applicability in other areas, students find the knowledge to be more meaningful. Additionally, utilizing concepts and skills in different contexts helps students to master and retain those skills. Cross-curricular instruction also aids students in their critical thinking skills such as inferring, drawing conclusions, predicting, and so forth. Cross-curricular instruction benefits teachers as well as students because it facilitates collaboration among colleagues. Teachers can plan together when lessons align across content areas and even team teach lessons.

Supporting Cross-Curricular Instruction

Leaders can support cross-curricular instruction by facilitating collaboration and providing resources for teachers. Cross-curricular instruction can be done independently but is more effective when teachers can collaborate in lesson planning. Leaders can provide time during the school day or at other times for teachers of different content areas to collaborate and examine the curriculum for opportunities for cross-curricular instruction. Also, leaders can support cross-curricular instruction by providing the appropriate resources. Teachers may have ideas that require books, supplies, or other materials to facilitate these lessons. Additionally, teachers may need training or professional development resources to help them present cross-curricular lessons effectively. Leaders can cultivate an environment where cross-curricular instruction is supported, encouraged, and praised.

Alignment of Curriculum and Instruction to Assessment

Curriculum and instruction must be aligned to assessment because what is taught must be measured and what is measured must be taught. If instruction is not aligned to the assessment, there will likely be no measurement of how well students mastered what was taught. Additionally, if instruction is not aligned to the assessment, students will likely be assessed on concepts and material they have not been taught. Neither scenario is fair or beneficial to students. In the case of district- or campus-created assessments, the assessment is often created first because this defines what students should know at the conclusion of the given time period. Then, based on the assessment's expectations, teachers can plan the order and pacing of the concepts and skills to teach. On state-mandated tests, students are expected to have mastered all skills and objectives provided by the state, but no one is aware of the test content until its administration.

Relationship Between Rigor and Differentiated Instruction

Rigorous instruction is challenging to students, but not impossible. However, classrooms are diverse and not all students perform at the same academic levels. As a result, teachers must provide an appropriate level of rigorous instruction to students based on their current performance. When teachers differentiate instruction for students, they cater to the individual needs of students, such as identifying the appropriate level of rigor for particular students or groups. For example, an eighth-grade math teacher would not give the same assignment to a struggling student as he or she would to a student who is performing above grade level. Each student needs a unique level of rigorous instruction. The teacher may identify that adding and subtracting fractions is a rigorous activity for the struggling student whereas the high-performing student may be able to solve algebraic equations that include fractions.

Relevance in Instruction

Relevance in instruction refers to how content is related to other content and to the real world, as experienced by the students in the classroom. When instruction is not relevant, students may have difficulty making connections to the instruction, identifying or connecting any background knowledge they may have, or retaining the information. In contrast, when instruction is relevant, students understand how the content connects to what they already know, what they are learning in other areas, and to the world around them. For example, a math teacher may explain to students how using an algebraic function can help them calculate their weekly paycheck on a job. An English teacher may compare a plot from classic literature to a modern-day movie or story to help students to make connections. Teachers make instruction relevant by demonstrating how the new content connects with old content, with the content they are learning in other courses, and with the real world as they experience it.

Supporting Student Engagement and Performance with Relevance in Instruction

When instruction is relevant to students, they are more likely to engage in it and demonstrate better academic performance. Students are better able to engage in relevant instruction because they understand how the new content relates to what they already know, which can build their interest and provide them with a way to contribute to the lesson. For example, if the students are reading a story in which a character spends a day at the beach, a student who has never been to the beach may have difficulty engaging in the lesson, whereas a student who has visited the beach is more eager to share experiences and connections to the lesson. Similarly, when students are taught abstract concepts, they may have difficulty grasping and retaining them if they are not relevant. In contrast, when students understand how concepts are applied in the real world, they are more likely to retain them. For example, students may learn about chemical reactions in a science course, but if they are shown how these chemical reactions occur in everyday life, such as cooking, they will have a deeper understanding of the concept and be more likely to retain it.

School-Wide Practices and Focus on Standards-Based Instruction

Differentiated Instruction

Differentiated instruction refers to providing customized or tailored instruction to students to meet their diverse learning needs. These learning needs can be determined by previous academic performance, special needs such as a physical or learning disability, learning style, or other means. Based on the identified needs, teachers can differentiate the content, process, or product of the instruction. When teachers differentiate content, they provide different content to students, such as a math teacher instructing one group of students on fractions and another group on algebraic equations. When teachers differentiate by process, a teacher provides different modes of instruction, such as video or media, field experiences, exploratory discovery, or other means. When a teacher differentiates by product, she provides different ways for students to demonstrate mastery of the content such as through writing, performance, or projects, among others. Teachers may differentiate instruction in all of these areas or in selected areas, based on the needs of the students.

Using Data to Support Differentiated Instruction

Instruction is differentiated based on students' needs. Data can be used to identify these needs, especially in the area of academic performance. Historical student performance data as well as current formative and summative assessments can help to determine the type of instruction a student may need. For example, the data may show that a certain group of students has deficits in reading. These students may benefit from not only reading a text, but additional methods of instructional delivery, as well as specific instruction that helps to build their reading skills. Data may inform campus leaders on what courses to offer. For example, if historical data demonstrates that many students have achieved advanced performance on state assessments, the leader may consider offering advanced classes in certain academic areas such as Advanced Placement, Gifted and Talented, Honors, and others. Other data that can be used to identify ways of differentiating instruction for students includes learning styles inventories, personality assessments, and observational data. These types of data can help teachers determine how to tailor instruction in a way that will support student learning and increase their academic performance.

Monitoring Curricular Programs to Ensure Student Needs and Content Standards Are Met

Monitoring Curricular Programs to Ensure They Are Meeting Student Needs

The school leader must monitor curricular programs to ensure that student needs are being met. If curricular programs do not meet student needs, students will not be successful and campus goals will not be met. The curricular program must meet the academic and social needs of students. For example, if a population of students on campus is consistently exceeding the performance standards on assessments, they need a curricular program that extends their learning and supports their academic growth. If the entire curricular program is centered on remediation, that group of students will not have their needs met. Campus leaders examine student needs and design the curricular program based on those needs. Such decisions may include which classes to offer, the uses of self-contained instruction or content-specific instruction, the offering of the arts and other ancillary instruction, the integration of tutorials and remediation into the school day, and many others.

Monitoring Curricular Programs to Ensure That They Meet Content Standards

The school leader must monitor curricular programs to ensure that they meet content standards. Content standards are determined by the state and are the basis for the design of state testing. Therefore, when curricular programs are not aligned to the content standards, students will not be prepared for state testing. If students are not prepared for state testing, they will not perform well and campus goals will not be met. Campus leaders must be mindful of how students will be assessed so that the curricular programs support instruction to adequately prepare students for those assessments. Additionally, ensuring that the campus curricular program meets content standards aids in vertical and horizontal alignment of instruction and curriculum both on campus and within the district. Vertical and horizontal alignment helps with collaborative planning among colleagues and ensures continuity of instruction for students, especially those with high mobility rates within the school district.

Effectively Monitoring the Curricular Program

Leaders can effectively monitor the curricular program by analyzing data, conducting observations, and soliciting feedback from stakeholders. If a curricular program is appropriate, student performance data in regard to content standards will be reflective of that. If students are not performing well, the campus leader may need to identify whether the curricular program has deficits or the programming is mismatched with student needs. Also, the leader can identify if the curricular program is working, based on observations of instruction on campus. For example, if the leader observes that students are demonstrating high levels of engagement in science courses, there may be an opportunity to expand the curricular program in science. Also, the leader can solicit feedback from stakeholders, such as teachers, students, and parents. These persons may identify needs or strengths of the curricular program for the leader to address. For example, Language Arts teachers may identify a need to separate reading and writing instruction in the curricular program to provide students with more time for instruction in these areas.

Ongoing Analyses for Quality of Teaching and Learning

Evaluating the Quality of Teaching on Campus

A school leader can evaluate the quality of teaching on campus through observations and data. A school leader should spend time in the classrooms to observe teaching in action. A school leader will recognize effective and ineffective teaching practices. It is important to observe teaching to evaluate quality so that if corrections are necessary, these can be made in time to affect student performance. After teaching has been completed, the school leader can analyze student performance data to evaluate the quality of the teaching. If teaching is of good quality, the majority of students should be able to grasp the concepts and demonstrate mastery on assessments. If many students are unable to master these concepts and objectives, teaching efficacy needs to be evaluated. School leaders can used both formative and summative assessments as indicators of teaching quality.

Evaluating the Quality of Learning on Campus

Student learning can be evaluated in a number of ways. A school leader can determine the quality of learning on campus through observations, feedback from students, and student performance data. When the school leader observes classroom instruction, he or she has the opportunity to observe students in the learning process. If students are excited about the content, are engaging significantly in the process, and are successful when checked for understanding, there is likely a high quality of learning. Also, a school leader may solicit feedback from students regarding their learning. This can be in the form of surveys, focus groups, or individual interviews. The students can be asked about the learning environment, the relevance of content, and the rigor of the instruction, among other quality indicators. Finally, a school leader needs to analyze student performance data to determine the quality of learning. If students are not meeting expectations on assessments, the quality of learning can likely be improved.

Benefits of Improving Teaching That Is Already Considered Effective

Even if teaching is deemed effective, there are still benefits to improving. Some school leaders focus solely on improving ineffective instruction, but that narrow focus results in a missed opportunity to develop and reinforce a culture of high expectations on campus. Effective instruction can become highly effective with additional support and strategies. When a school leader is committed to improving all instruction on campus, even instruction that is considered effective, all staff are encouraged to grow professionally for the benefit of students. This fosters an environment of continuous improvement and also helps teachers to seek changes in the instructional program and in student diversity. This environment also encourages innovation in the classroom to find new and creative ways for instructing learners. Also, increasing the effectiveness of teaching can help high-performing students to grow and perform at even higher academic levels.

Addressing Teaching That Is Not Effective

It is a school leader's responsibility to address ineffective teaching. First, the leader must identify the ineffective teaching. This is done through observations of classroom instruction and review of student performance. Next, a leader must communicate to the teacher which aspects of the instruction are ineffective. A leader should be strategic in communicating areas of improvement to avoid discouraging the teacher and to focus the teacher's growth in the areas that will have the most impact on students. Then, the leader must provide the resources and support to improve the ineffective teaching. This can include professional development and instructional coaching. The leader should also continue to monitor instruction to determine if improvements are being made. In some instances, depending on the severity of the deficits in instruction, the school leader may decide to change staff's instructional assignments or even remove staff from their assignments. If staff is changed or removed, the school leader must adhere to district policies regarding staff changes.

Formative and Summative Assessment, Effective Teaching, and Program Quality

Formative Assessment

Formative assessment is designed to monitor student learning. Formative assessment is useful in providing feedback to students so they will know which areas they need to improve and so teachers will also know areas in which to improve their teaching. The results of formative assessment may help teachers identify instructional areas for re-teaching or identify students for interventions and tutorials. Formative assessment may include checks for understanding within the classroom, classroom activities, and other guided and independent work. Formative assessments are usually activities that are low stakes, meaning that often no grade or point value is attached. For example, a teacher may ask students to represent their understanding of a concept using a graphic organizer. A teacher may also provide feedback on a pre-writing activity before a student writes an essay. Formative assessment may occur frequently and feedback should be timely in order to be relevant.

Summative Assessment

Summative assessment is used to evaluate student learning for mastery. Summative assessment usually occurs at the end of an instructional unit or a designated period of time such as a grading period or school year. These assessments are aligned to objectives or standards and are usually high stakes, which means they may count for a significant portion of the grade or may determine a students' progress in their educational careers. A summative assessment may be a midterm or final exam, a research project, a unit test, or a standardized exam. The results of summative assessments may determine a student's grade promotion or earning of course credit. Results from summative assessment may also determine a school's performance according to accountability standards. Summative assessment results are often used by school leaders for instructional planning and goal-setting for the subsequent school year.

Indicators of Effective Teaching

A leader can use several indicators to identify effective teaching on campus. With effective teaching, there is a clear goal or objective to be accomplished with the instruction. This objective is communicated to students and is evident throughout the lesson. Additionally, there is a clear lesson cycle throughout the instructional delivery, such as a gradual release teaching model in which students are supported throughout the learning process. When there is effective teaching, students are engaged in the learning and demonstrate retention of the concepts through formative assessment. Effective instruction includes diverse instructional strategies to meet the needs of learners and is responsive to the results of the formative assessment conducted in the classroom. Also, effective teaching is evident in student performance data. Students who receive effective instruction are able to perform to standard on assessments.

Assessing Program Quality

A leader can assess program quality using data and feedback from stakeholders. Data that can inform a leader regarding program quality includes participation or attendance data, student performance data, and any other metrics that are collected, such as those specified by grants or state and national associations. If a program is good quality, parents and community members will participate in it, which is reflected in the participation and attendance data. Also, student performance will reflect whether a program is high quality. If student performance is below standard, this may be an indicator that the school's programming may be misaligned or below standard. Other metrics dictated by outside agencies may include the data relating to parent and community events, awards received, college acceptance, and others. A leader can also obtain feedback from stakeholders. Teachers, staff, students, and community members will generally be pleased with the implementation of a high quality program. Low approval of the school's program may suggest that the leader needs to examine its appropriateness on campus or its implementation.

Alternative Assessment Methods

Traditional methods of assessment usually involve a standardized test with closed questions, which require students to select an answer from several choices. Educators are now trying to incorporate a greater variety of assessment methods so that students can demonstrate mastery of content and objectives in different ways. These alternative methods may include writing assessments, project assessments, and performance assessments. Writing assessments may include responding to open-ended questions or writing an essay or work of fiction. Project assessments typically require students to conduct extensive research and compile a final product with multiple parts or aspects. Project assessments have typically been used in science and social studies courses but are now being incorporated across the curriculum. Performance assessments require the student to perform in front of peers or the teacher. These may include a speech, skit, dance, or some other physical demonstration of their learning. Many of these alternative assessments are also facilitated using technology applications.

Two-Way Communication About Progress Toward Goals

Communicating with Staff

It is important for a school leader to communicate with staff about progress toward goals to maintain or increase momentum, as well as to celebrate successes. A leader can communicate with staff about progress toward goals through the normal channels: emails, employee newsletters, or staff meetings. Incorporating goal progress within these forms of communication helps the staff to view goal progress as something that is as important as the other topics that are being communicated. Also, it does not require staff to utilize a new or foreign form of communication to determine progress toward goals. However, a leader may want to publicize progress in more public or visible ways. These may include public announcements, posters or charts in hallways and meeting rooms, or special charts and graphs that can be shared with staff. Reaching goals or goal milestones can also be celebrated with awards, certificates, or other means.

Communicating with Parents and Community

A leader should communicate with parents and community about goal progress often and in a variety of ways. This can include community meetings in which stakeholders are invited to hear about school performance in a variety of areas, with a focus on goals. Additionally, the leader can provide a newsletter or bulletin to update the community on school performance, upcoming events, and ways to get involved with the school to help achieve the goals. Many schools feature phone systems that can mass call the homes of students, which can be used to communicate announcements regarding school goals and progress toward them. Similarly, school leaders can mail letters to parents with updates regarding the school goals. Progress toward school goals can also be communicated in other meetings that involve parents and community members, such as committee meetings, parent teacher organization meetings, and advisory board meetings.

Communicating with Students

Teachers can communicate with students about the school's goals and how their individual efforts and performance contribute toward achieving them. For goals that are related to student academic performance, teachers can help students take ownership of their own performance by setting individual goals and tracking their progress toward them. Students can be provided with data trackers to track their own progress toward their individual goals. Teachers can speak with students individually about the support they need to accomplish their goals. Teachers can also set class goals that align with campus goals and encourage students to reach them. For example, if the school has a goal of 90% proficiency in math performance, a math teacher can help students set individual goals in math. This ensures that students understand how their behaviors affect their class and school and demonstrates how they can contribute to the school's success while achieving their own success.

Importance of Facilitating Two-Way Communication

Two-way communication on progress toward goals is important because it provides stakeholders with the opportunity to convey to the leader why goals may or may not be achieved. When a leader facilitates two-way communication, he or she can receive feedback on the efficacy of existing strategies, ideas for additional strategies, or requests for additional resources or support. For example, if the campus has a goal to increase student proficiency in technology and the leader has purchased certain technology hardware to accomplish this goal, teachers may provide feedback that the chosen hardware has not been effective in exposing students to technology and that another type of hardware may be necessary. Additionally, two-way communication may reveal unexpected barriers to achieving goals. For example, a teacher may inform the leader that the technology goal may be difficult to achieve because the school technology infrastructure cannot support the increased Internet usage on campus. A leader can benefit from two-way communication about progress toward goals by receiving additional information that can lead to refining or revising goals, or that assures the leader that the right actions have been implemented.

School Improvement Leadership

Models of Leadership

Impact of a Leader's Personal Values and Beliefs on the Effectiveness of Leadership

A leader's personal values and beliefs shape his or her behavior, as well as expectations from staff and students. One's personal beliefs will dictate what is prioritized as a leader and as a campus team. If the leader's values and beliefs reflect positive attributes, these can have a positive impact on the effectiveness of leadership. In contrast, if the leader's beliefs and values are contrary to district and community norms, these can make it difficult to lead effectively. Additionally, if staff members have values and beliefs that are contrary to the leader's, they may find it difficult to follow the leader. For example, if the leader values reading and believes that everyone should be an avid reader, he or she would likely emphasize and prioritize reading initiatives and be effective in promoting reading on campus. On the other hand, if a leader did not personally value a characteristic such as punctuality in staff and students, that leader may have difficult effectively enforcing promptness among staff and students on campus. The leader's values and beliefs are often demonstrated in the school mission and vision, as well as through the leader's words and actions.

Acting as a Role Model

People observe the leader's behavior for alignment between his or her words and actions. This alignment is necessary for a leader to be viewed as genuine and authentic. The leader serves as a role model for both staff and students. For staff, the leader should exemplify the mission and vision of the school through behavior and words. The leader should also set the example in adhering to campus and district policy, like those described in the employee handbook. Additionally, the leader should set the example for campus culture, such as how staff members treat one another and students. For students, the leader is a role model in dress, conduct, speech, and other areas. Many people in the community may look up to the leader as well as an example to follow. As a role model, the leader's behavior can influence the behavior of others as he or she comes into contact with them.

Servant Leader

A servant leader is a person who leads by serving others first. A servant leader identifies the team's needs by assessing the team or listening to team members and then meets those needs. Meeting the team's needs helps to equip them to get their job done effectively and efficiently. A servant leader shares power through empowering others to be effective and by providing them with the tools and resources to be effective. This is in contrast to a leader who exerts authority over others in a "top-down" approach. A servant leader is often found participating in the work with the team, both to support the team and to experience the team members' jobs. A faculty with a servant leader is more likely to feel more confident in their ability to do their job because their leader has empowered and equipped them and does not micromanage their work. Servant leaders are often described as caring, compassionate, thoughtful, and humble.

Transactional vs. Transformational Leadership Styles

Transactional and transformational leadership styles are very different and produce different results from team members. Transactional leaders are most concerned about how to effectively implement and perform under the current rules, policies, and procedures, whereas transformational leaders are focused on change and improvement. Transactional leaders emphasize compliance and monitor progress toward goals using systems of rewards and punishment. These leaders can be task-oriented or focused on results only. These types of leaders can become micromanagers. In contrast, transformational leaders focus on the staff behaviors that lead to success. They focus on organizational values and implementation of the mission and vision in order to meet goals. These types of leaders focus on growing staff members in order to meet goals and solicit staff buy-in in the decision-making process. There are pros and cons of each leadership style and many leaders alternate between these leadership styles or blend them together in order to lead effectively.

Shared Leadership

Shared leadership is the delegation of authority and responsibility to other team members. This type of leadership is the opposite of authoritarian leadership or micromanaging. Instead, a leader will appoint persons with particular leadership responsibilities and grant them the authority to fulfill those responsibilities. For example, the school leader may ask a skilled teacher to lead a curriculum revision process and supervise a group of other teachers on the task. When sharing leadership, responsibility can be delegated to any staff persons who are capable of fulfilling the role. It is not dependent on job titles. Shared leadership also involves including team members in the leader's decision-making processes. This means that the school leader may solicit opinions, ideas, and feedback from staff members before making a decision. This can be accomplished through focus groups, appointing advisors, or taking votes during meetings.

Using a Variety of Roles to Accomplish Vision

Campus Roles That Can Help Accomplish the Vision

Many roles are performed on campus to ensure that day-to-day activities are carried out. Each of these roles can contribute to accomplishing the school vision. Some of the roles include the administrative team, school counselors, teacher leaders, and support staff. The administrative team is essential in accomplishing the vision because projects and assignments that directly impact the vision and school goals can be delegated to them. These administrators have the authority and training to support the leader in leading the campus to success. School counselors can help accomplish the vision by supporting the psychosocial needs of students so that they can be their best, academically and socially. School counselors are often part of the team that handles student scheduling and post-graduation plans, so they can help students meet the expectations associated with campus goals. Teacher leaders can also help to accomplish the vision by leading, encouraging, and supporting their fellow teachers. Finally, support staff can help accomplish the vision by ensuring that plan logistics are appropriate, communication is timely and effective, and staff and stakeholders feel supported and equipped to implement the vision.

Distributing Responsibility and the Role of Shared Vision

Helping Goal Implementation with a Shared Vision

A vision can be shared in two ways. In the development of a vision, the leader can solicit the opinions and feedback of stakeholders so that a variety of perspectives, opinions, and beliefs can be incorporated into the vision. When the vision is developed in this manner, participants can see their contribution to the vision by the way that it is articulated and implemented. A vision is also shared when a leader effectively communicates the vision, the rationale for the vision, and the plans for implementing the vision to stakeholders. When a vision is shared, this can assist with goal implementation because of buy-in from stakeholders. People are more willing to agree with and participate in plans that they helped to develop. Additionally, having a shared vision means that stakeholders will understand it well enough to work toward goal implementation, even without direct supervision from the leader. They will be able to take action to advance toward the campus goals.

Importance of Delegating Tasks and Responsibilities

Leading a campus is a great responsibility that cannot be done alone. To lead effectively, a leader must delegate tasks and responsibilities. Delegation is important because a leader does not have the time or resources to perform all responsibilities alone. Most initiatives require a team of people to get the job done in a timely and efficient manner. Delegation is also important because a leader will not have all of the skills necessary to perform every task. For example, a project may require computer networking expertise, which the leader may not have. In order for projects to be completely effectively, tasks and responsibilities should be delegated according to skillsets. Delegation is also important because there are tasks and responsibilities that only the leader can perform, so his or her time should prioritize these types of activities. Other activities that can be accomplished by other team members should be delegated whenever possible. Delegation also ensures that the campus will run efficiently in the absence of the leader, such as during a meeting or other event.

Relationship Between Delegation and Accountability

For delegation to be effective, a leader must hold team members accountable. A leader cannot delegate tasks and responsibilities without checking on the progress, or he or she may discover too late that the job was not done or did not meet expectations. Instead, a leader can incorporate accountability into delegation. This can be done by setting regular check-in dates with team members to meet about task progress, providing the leader with an opportunity to give feedback. The leader can also set certain milestones that must be accomplished to demonstrate progress. The leader should emphasize to the team member that completion of the project is his or her responsibility and that completion is a reflection of job performance. When a leader includes accountability through regular check-ins, pre-established milestones, and communication of responsibility, the team member will be clear about expectations and able to perform the delegated task, and the leader will be reassured that the job is being completed to satisfaction.

Relationship Between Delegation and Authority

For effective delegation of tasks and responsibilities, those responsible must have the appropriate authority to accomplish the tasks. Often, the projects that need to be delegated are not ones that can be done independently. They require the coordination of other people and resources. It may be necessary for the school leader to expressly communicate to the person to whom the task is delegated as well as those assisting that the project leader has the authority to implement the project. This will help those leading the project to have confidence in their ability to get the job done. For example, if a project requires the scheduling of a community meeting, the project leader would need the authority to secure the venue, make purchases, and gather volunteers for the event. Providing team members with authority enables them to accomplish their delegated tasks with little to no dependence on the school leader. In contrast, when a project leader does not have the appropriate authority to get the project done, the project could be delayed or remain incomplete, waiting on assistance from the school leader.

Monitoring and Communicating About Progress Toward the Goal

Effectively Monitoring Goal Progress

A leader effectively monitors goal progress by implementing clear checkpoints and milestones in goal activities. Each goal should be broken down into smaller goals, or milestones, that can be reviewed in regular intervals. This allows the leader to analyze progress toward the goal in a timely manner so that, if progress is insufficient, there is time to intervene and make changes to the action steps. For example, if the campus goal is to achieve a 90% passing rate on reading assessments for third-grade students, the campus leader would want established milestones to monitor reading progress throughout the school year. The leader may review reading data every three weeks to determine if third-grade students are reaching and maintaining a 90% passing rate in reading. If not, the leader could implement additional strategies to increase the support for reading instruction. Checkpoints for goals are often aligned with grading periods, as identified on the school academic calendar.

Effectively Communicating Goal Progress

Goal progress should be communicated effectively and in a timely manner, especially to those who are instrumental in achieving the goal. First, the school leader should monitor goal progress closely so that it can be communicated in a timely manner. Communicating goal progress is pointless if it is done with no time left to make adjustments. The school leader should communicate progress consistently, whether positive or negative. Communicating positive goal progress is encouraging to others and reassures them that their actions are appropriate. This can serve as positive reinforcement that may even increase staff performance. In contrast, communicating negative goal progress is necessary so that corrections can be made. When communicating goal progress, conducting in-person conversations or meetings is beneficial because it allows for two-way communication. During these conversations, the school leader may discover unexpected barriers and challenges that need to be addressed.

Adjusting Vision, Goals, Implementation, and Communication Strategies

Continuous Improvement

The process of continuous improvement is the ongoing act of assessing performance and adjusting efforts to improve that importance. With a process of continuous improvement, parts of the work process can be addressed before they begin to fail. Low-performing processes are improved as well as performance that is considered acceptable. All aspects of the work process are examined to determine where improvements can be made to reach excellence. To implement a process of continuous improvement, procedures of evaluation must be developed and implemented at regular checkpoints. Based on these evaluations, the leadership team can identify areas of improvement and initiate interventions and actions based on these areas. In schools, the regular evaluation of process toward the campus vision and goals can be developed into a process of continuous improvement. However, campus leaders must focus on both the strengths and weaknesses of the campus in this process. Deficient areas can be improved to perform to standard and areas performing at standard can be innovated for improvement.

Effectively Monitor Progress

A leader can effectively monitor progress by planning regular checkpoints, analyzing data, and actively engaging in the work. The leader must plan in advance when to check progress on the projects and tasks that are being implemented on campus. This monitoring should include the projects that the leader is working on as well as those that have been delegated to others. These checkpoints should occur with enough frequency that adjustments can be made in a timely manner. The leader must also analyze data on a regular basis. All goals should have measurable metrics, which means that data points can demonstrate whether the goal is on track to be achieved. Therefore, a leader must be skilled at analyzing data and making decisions based on it. Finally, a leader can effectively monitor progress by viewing the work and engaging in it firsthand. For example, if a campus goal is to reduce the number of students who are tardy, the school leader may engage in morning duty to monitor the arrival and attendance tracking of students. This engagement can add context to the data and help the leader to identify areas of improvement.

Facilitating Self-Directed Change and Improvement on Campus

Self-directed change and improvement can help achieve the campus vision and goals. Staff members who can make changes and improvement to their practice on their own do not require as much intervention of campus leaders and coaches as other staff members, freeing those resources to be utilized in other areas. To succeed on their own, staff members must be fully aware of the campus visions and goals and the expectations placed on them in pursuit of those goals. A leader can facilitate self-directed change and improvement by providing adequate staff resources, such as instructional resources and professional development opportunities. The leader must also provide staff members with access to data for monitoring progress and performance. Finally, the leader must develop a culture and climate of self-improvement in which staff are comfortable revealing weaknesses and taking risks to improve their practice.

Helping with Adjustment of the Vision and Goals by Self-Reflection

Self-reflection is the process of examining one's self in relation to a desired expectation of performance. This process can help with adjusting the vision and goals when it is completed by those responsible for carrying out tasks and projects related to the vision and goals. Self-reflection can help to determine whether the goals should be revised or if they or persons striving toward the goals need improvement. For example, if a campus goal is to improve reading instruction, reading teachers could engage in self-reflection to determine if they are implementing the action plan with fidelity and are teaching to their best ability. If not, the teachers would engage in self-directed change to meet the goal. In contrast, if the reading teachers were faithfully implementing the action plan and performing to the best of their ability, this could indicate that the goal itself and its associated strategies may require revision to meet the students' needs. When all staff members engage in self-reflection, it becomes easier for the campus as a whole to make changes and improve.

Systematically Reviewing and Revising Goals

Goals are not concrete and should be reviewed and revised periodically. A leader can examine goals to determine whether a campus is likely to achieve or exceed them. A leader can also determine whether goals are in complete alignment with the vision of the schools. Just as a leader regularly monitors the activities implemented for the completion of the goal, the leader will need to examine the goals themselves. Since a goal is measurable, the leader can determine if the current data shows that the campus is on track for meeting it. The leader may observe unexpected barriers to achieving the goal that require a revision or the setting of an additional goal. For example, if the school sets a goal for reading performance, the leader may notice that students receiving special education services are not performing as well as students who do not receive these services, and that their reading performance is contributing to a low overall reading performance goal. The leader may then create a new goal that specifically addresses the needs of this student population with its own set of strategies and interventions.

Determining If Communication Strategies Need to Be Adjusted

Communication of the vision and goals to all stakeholders is critical to the successful achievement of the vision and goals. The leader will know that communication strategies need to be adjusted if staff members have difficulty articulating or implementing the goals and vision. All staff members should be able to discuss the campus goals and vision among themselves and with other stakeholders. If they are unable to do this, it is possible that communication was not effective initially or that subsequent communication of changes and adjustments to the vision and goals was ineffective. Another indication that communication strategies need adjustment is difficulty for staff members in implementing the action plans related to the vision and goals. If they are unclear about what is expected of them or what steps they need to take to meet expectations, these aspects of the action plan may not have been conveyed clearly. Communicating effectively removes barriers to implementation.

Gathering Data and Identifying Strong and Weak Areas

Identifying Strengths and Weaknesses of Campus Performance

The school leader can use quantitative, anecdotal, and observation data to identify the strengths and weaknesses of campus performance. This involves regular reporting of student performance data and other data points related to key areas such as attendance and discipline. This data is usually analyzed in relation to goal setting and review of goals, so leaders can actively identify the strengths and weaknesses of the campus when this data is reviewed. Also, other team members or district office personal might convey areas of strength or weakness to the leaders based on their campus experiences. These persons may share how a particular teacher or department is performing or provide feedback regarding a system or process on campus. Also, a leader may make observations on campus to help identify areas of strength or needed improvement. For example, a leader may participate in lunch duty in the cafeteria and observe processes that need to be improved. A leader should refer to multiple sources of data and evidence to develop a holistic view of the strengths and weaknesses of campus performance.

Addressing Identified Strengths on Campus

A leader should address identified strengths on campus by using them as opportunities for praise and reinforcement, as well as leverage for improvement. Effective leaders encourage staff by praising and celebrating achievements and recognizing strengths. This motivates staff members to continue the effective performance. For strengths to remain as strengths, a leader must recognize them and reinforce the actions and attitudes that led to their achievement. The leader can also use these strengths as leverage for making improvements. For example, if the third-grade reading teachers have consistently achieved high performance in reading, this can be recognized and praised. Then the strategies that these teachers implement in the third-grade classroom can be analyzed for application to the other grade levels. Reinforcing and praising strengths builds confidence in team members, helping them to address needed improvements on campus. Similarly, the skills that are effective in building the strengths can also be applied to areas of weakness.

Addressing Identified Weaknesses on Campus

Weaknesses identified on campus must be addressed to improve them. However, this should be done strategically to avoid demoralizing team members. If a leader identifies multiple weaknesses, they can be prioritized rather than attempting to address all of the weaknesses at once. Attempting to address all at one time can be overwhelming to team members. When developing plans to address weaknesses, the leader needs to identify how the strengths of the campus and the individual team members can be used to improve the areas of weakness. For example, a campus may be having difficulty with classroom management, but certain teachers may be effective classroom managers. These teachers can be used to develop a campus-wide strategy for addressing this area of weakness. Similarly, the campus may demonstrate weakness in math performance, but strength in reading performance. The campus leader can identify the strategies that make reading performance effective and implement them in math instruction.

Using School Accountability Measures to Identify Strengths and Weaknesses

The purpose of school accountability measures is to ensure that all students are learning and performing according to predetermined standards. These measures of accountability are standardized and the state and federal governments provide assessments of schools based on these accountability standards. School leaders can use these school reports to identify areas of strength and weakness in the school programming as measured by performance on state-mandated assessments. For example, the school leader may review the school's accountability ratings and find that the third-grade class did not perform according to expectations in reading. Based on that information, the leader can identify which teachers taught third-grade reading, what curriculum was used, and other factors that may have impacted students' scores. That information can then be used to determine what aspects of the third-grade reading program are strong and which are weak and need improvement. School accountability measures are a critical means of determining a school's strengths and weaknesses.

Implementing Change

Professional Development

To implement change, identifying areas for improvement is not enough. Staff members need to know what they can do to improve their practice. As a result, professional development can help a leader implement change. When leaders participate in professional development themselves, they can learn how to be better leaders and how to implement new or better instructional practices on campus. When teachers and other staff participate in professional development, they can also learn how to grow as professionals and implement improved instructional strategies in the classroom. Leaders should tailor professional development to meet the needs of the staff and to address campus weaknesses. Leaders should also offer opportunities for staff members to participate in individualized and group professional development, organized by content area, grade level, or shared strengths or weaknesses. Also, leaders should implement professional development in innovative ways, such as coaching, modeling, book talks, and other professional development strategies.

Studying Research-Based and Proven Best Practices

Areas of deficit or weakness on campus often result from a lack of knowledge rather than a lack of capability. Leaders and team members must continually learn about their practice and how they can improve, and should search for successful strategies that can be implemented on their campus. To address weak areas, it is better to implement strategies that are backed by research and have been proven to obtain good results. This can save the campus the time, effort, and resources that could be wasted if untested, unproven strategies are implemented unsuccessfully. When a leader is looking for strategies to foster change on campus, using research-based, proven best practices is beneficial because there will be clear direction for successfully implementing the strategy as well as an idea of the expected results. When untested strategies are implemented, the outcome is less sure. Untested strategies also often take more research and a process of trial and error to implement, also known as a learning curve, both of which can delay the implementation of change.

Enlisting Support for Change on Campus

A leader cannot bring about campus change alone. To make changes happen, the leader must enlist support. Fostering change as a change agent requires leaders to be strategic in how they communicate the change and how they garner supporters for it. First, the leader needs to communicate the change effectively. Many people are unwilling to support changes because they fear the unknown. The leader should not only communicate what is to be changed, but also how it will affect the various staff members and how they are aligned to the vision and goals. Next, the leader needs to gather other leaders within the team and persuade them to support the change. Leaders on campus may carry official titles of leadership or simply have influence over other staff members. Enlisting the support of these persons will positively affect the perceptions of the remaining staff. Lastly, the leader needs to be a constant advocate of change and participate in it. Staff members will watch the leader to see if the desire for change is authentic and long-lasting. They will be more likely to support it when they observe that the leader is serious about change.

Anticipating and Preparing for When to Implement Change

When implementing change, a school leader should anticipate and prepare for varying levels of support, as well as direct opposition to the change. Some team members will be as enthusiastic about the change as the leader. The leader should be prepared to leverage these team members by encouraging them, providing them with resources necessary to implement the changes, and using them to influence the other team members. Some team members will be indecisive about the change and not quite ready to support it. The leader should be prepared to spend more time and resources on this group to help encourage them to support the change. This group may require additional communication strategies and support to bring them on board. The school leader should also anticipate a third group of staff members who are opposed to the change and may even be vocal in their opposition. The school leader should be prepared to defend the change and offer rebuttals to arguments against it, both publicly and privately. The majority of the leader's focus should be on the first two groups; however, the oppositional group can be detrimental to the progress of the first two groups if it is not addressed appropriately.

Modeling Openness to Change

The leader is a model on campus and team members will imitate his or her attitudes. If a leader would like the staff to be open to proposed change, he or she must also be a model of openness to change. There are many ways to accomplish a goal, and just because something is working does not mean that it cannot be improved. Changes may be proposed by team members other than the leader, from the school district, or even from the state. In these instances, the leader should model openness to change. The leader can be receptive to the proposed change and optimistic as to how the change can positively affect the campus. The leader can also demonstrate a positive attitude during the change, should it be implemented. The leader can expect a similar response from staff if change is proposed on campus, so leadership should model the qualities and attitudes they desire from staff. In contrast, if the leader is not open to change, staff will likely imitate that attitude and be opposed to changes proposed by the leader.

Integrity

Integrity refers to being honest and trustworthy and exhibiting moral principles. A person with integrity is generally of good character. A school leader can demonstrate integrity by behaving in a trustworthy manner with district personnel, staff, students, parents, and community stakeholders. The school leader should behave ethically in regard to all aspects of the position, including finance, personnel issues, and student matters. A school leader with integrity will hold him or herself and others accountable for ethical behavior, will recognize when ethics have been breached, and will take appropriate action in response. A school leader will also implement systems and procedures to ensure that the rights and confidentiality of students and staff are maintained at all times.

When a Situation Presents a Conflict of Interest

A conflict of interest is a situation in which the school leader can obtain personal gain or harm from a decision made as a leader. For example, a school leader may determine that the school gymnasium needs to be repainted. A family member of the leader owns a company that provides such a service and offers a bid. This would present a conflict of interest for the leader because he or she would potentially derive a benefit from hiring a family member's business to complete the job. Other situations that could present a conflict of interest may include hiring or terminating staff, awarding or disciplining a student who is a family member, or voting in an official capacity for colleagues or family members. A school leader should be aware of potential conflicts of interest and alert superiors should such a situation arise.

How Laws and Regulations Protect Privacy and Confidentiality of Information

Laws and regulations have been enacted to protect the privacy and confidentiality of students and staff in schools. Specifically, the Family Educational Rights and Privacy Act (FERPA) is a federal law that protects the privacy of student education records. Any school that receives funds from the United States Department of Education is subject to this law. It provides guidelines for who can access or view student records, who can alter student records, and what student information can be disseminated without student or parental consent. School leaders must abide by this law and implement policies and procedures on campus that ensure other school personnel also abide by this law. Additionally, schools have the obligation to inform parents and students aged 18 or older of their rights under FERPA.

Situations Involving Issues of Ethics and Integrity

A school leader will find that many of the situations they encounter involve issues of ethics and integrity. These situations may involve students, parents, personnel, and community members. Situations regarding students may involve grades, retention or promotion, assigning consequences in discipline matters, awards and recognition, and others. Situations involving parents may be student related or involve fundraising, elections to committees, or others. Situations regarding personnel may involve reprimands or other discipline, promotions, pay, and others. Additionally, situations involving community members may involve voting and elections, awarding contracts, exchanging services, and more. The leader must also use ethics and integrity in their own decision-making processes in regard to budgeting, school academic and extracurricular programming, and business and community partnerships.

Elements of a Transparent Decision-Making Process

Some school decisions require input from stakeholders. In these decisions, it is important to have a transparent decision-making process so that all stakeholders can be assured that the decision is made ethically and with integrity. First, stakeholders must be notified in advance of the decision to be made. They should also have access to relevant information for making the decision, in accordance with any privacy or confidentiality regulations. They should be notified in advance of any public meetings related to the decision and documented meeting minutes should be made available. Any voting related to the decision should also be documented for transparency. Finally, when the school leader has made a decision, it should be shared with stakeholders along with the rationale for it, such as community input, votes, and other information.

Ensuring Equitable Treatment of Students and Staff

The best way that the school leader can ensure equitable treatment of students and staff is to develop policies and procedures and adhere to them. When there are policies and procedures in place, the school leader can refer to these to determine the best course of action when dealing with students and staff. For example, if a student has excessive school absences, a school attendance policy should dictate when and how to address absenteeism. Similarly, if a staff member dresses unprofessionally for work, an employee handbook should outline how to address the staff member. In a situation with no guiding policy, the school leader should use discretion in handling the situation and subsequently develop a guiding policy for future incidents. This can be in the form of memorandums or addendums to existing student and staff handbooks. While there may be extenuating circumstances that require the school leader's discretion, policies and procedures ensure that all are treated equitably.

Ensuring That Others Are Acting Ethically

A leader can ensure that others are acting ethically by communicating expectations regarding ethical behavior. The leader can provide staff with documents and training that explain these expectations. Employees should acknowledge receipt of such documentation by signing to confirm that they have received them as well as signing in at training sessions to confirm participation. The leader can also monitor employee behavior. This can be done in person by walking around and observing performance or remotely by instructing others on the leadership team to observe employee behavior or monitoring with security cameras. Security cameras are useful in areas that are most prone to unethical conduct, such as places where money is exchanged, entrances and exits, records storage, and areas on campus that are not frequently trafficked. Additionally, the leader can implement consequences for unethical behavior and address such behavior swiftly. Employees may be encouraged to behave ethically to avoid consequences for unethical behavior.

Consequences of Unethical Behavior

Consequences for an employee's unethical behavior can vary, depending on the severity of the offense. For a minor offense, the employee may receive a verbal or written reprimand to be included in his or her personnel file. This type of situation may require a formal conference with the school leader or other school district staff. More severe offenses can result in suspension, reassignment, or termination of employment. For example, if an employee has behaved in an unethical manner involving exchange of money, he or she may be reassigned to a position that does not require interaction with money. Severe offenses can result in the suspension or revocation of state licensure. Ethical offenses that involve breaking the law can also result in legal consequences such as fines, probation, or even imprisonment as determined by city, state, and federal law.

Steps to Take When Ethics Have Been Breached

If a school leader has been made aware of an ethical violation, it is his or her responsibility to act immediately. In many cases, there are procedures or guidelines that a school leader should follow, as determined by the school district. These procedures may include notifying district personnel, initiating an investigation, conferencing with the offending employee, drafting a formal note of reprimand, or other actions. There should also be guidance from the school district on notifying outside authorities or organizations, such as law enforcement or Child Protective Services. In some instances, district personnel or an entity acting on their behalf handle the situation and the school leader takes on a role of support and facilitation. It is important for a school leader to take reports of unethical behavior seriously and act quickly and appropriately. Additionally, the school leader should maintain thorough documentation of the events and timelines for audit purposes.

Justice and Fairness

Social Justice

Social justice refers to the fair and equitable treatment of all persons, regardless of their status in society. Factors such as socioeconomic status, race, ethnicity, place of residence, and others influence the privileges that certain persons may have in society. These privileges, or lack thereof, can be reflected in the school system as well. The concept of social justice as it relates to education means that all students, regardless of their social status, socioeconomic status, race, ethnicity, religion, sexual orientation, or any other identifying factor, are entitled to an equitable education and access to educational resources. For example, it is considered a social injustice for children in poverty to have outdated textbooks and a lack of access to technology in schools. Social justice in education refers to advocating for children who are typically marginalized and disenfranchised so that they can receive the same educational opportunities as other children.

Advocating for All Children

A school leader is in a unique position to be an advocate for all children on campus. First, the school leader needs to ensure that the academic and extracurricular programming is accessible to all children and reflective of the needs of all children on campus. Next, the school leader should ensure that all special programming is properly funded and implemented on campus. This can include programs such as Title I, special education, gifted and talented programs, English as a Second Language programs, career and technology programs, and many others. Finally, some inequities are the result of governmental policy, which affect the school. The school leader can use his or her voice and authority to influence policy and promote social justice in the school. Examples of these types of policy issues include school finance and funding, school zoning, school vouchers, and many others.

Communication of Expectations for the Staff and Students

Importance of Communicating Expectations to Staff and Students

The school leader must communicate expectations to staff and students to increase the likelihood that staff and students will meet those expectations. It is difficult for staff and students to meet expectations if they are unaware of them. This can result in unintentional disregard of expectations. For example, teachers may decide to leave campus during an instructional planning period. If the teachers are unaware that the school leader expects them to remain on campus even when they do not have class, it will be difficult for the school leader to hold them accountable for that behavior. Likewise, the school leader should communicate expectations of behavior to students before a presumed offense is committed. A school leader must effectively communicate expectations so that students and staff will know what behavior to demonstrate and so the school leader can hold them accountable for those behaviors.

Communicating Expectations to Staff and Students

A school leader has many opportunities to communicate expectations to staff and students. These expectations can be written and shared in employee and student handbooks or codes of conduct. These documents can be printed as well as made available online. The school leader may require that staff and students provide a signature acknowledging receipt of such documents. Additionally, expectations for behavior can be communicated or reinforced during announcements, in assemblies or meetings, and in individual conversations. Many school leaders post expectations for behavior on posters in school hallways and classrooms. These often take the form of classroom rules for behavior, hallway expectations, cafeteria expectations, and so on. When correcting behavior that does not meet expectations, the school leader can reinforce expectations for the offender. For example, the school leader may verbalize to an employee that he or she is late to work and remind him or her of the expected arrival time.

Appropriateness and Efficacy of System for Protecting and Advocating for Students

Determining the Appropriateness/Efficacy of Systems for Protecting and Advocating for Students

A school leader should have systems in place for the protection and advocacy of students. These systems should be based on the needs of the student population and should be responsive to the changing needs and concerns of these students. A school leader will know if these systems are appropriate and effective in various ways. First, there should be a student culture of safety in school. This culture involves students feeling free to engage in the academic program, social activities, and extracurricular activities. Also, students should have an adequate voice. An appropriate and effective system for protection and advocacy will allow various avenues for students to contribute their ideas and voice their concerns. Additionally, there will be evidence that students are supported in times of need or crisis. This means that socio-emotional needs are identified and addressed quickly so that students can engage in the school program. These systems are effective and appropriate only if they benefit all students. If some groups of students are marginalized or neglected on campus, the school leader must revisit the appropriateness and efficacy of the school's systems.

Potential Opportunities to Serve as an Advocate for Students

Advocacy for students is necessary whenever any group of students is or has the potential to be marginalized. These groups are commonly students of low socioeconomic status, minority status, immigrant status, or a different sexual orientation. However, any student or group of students can need advocacy at any given time. There is an opportunity to advocate for these students when their right to an equitable education in a safe environment is threatened. For example, a school leader may observe that an academic program offered in the district consistently leaves out students who receive special education services. The school leader may advocate for that group of students by calling for a review of the application and acceptance criteria to drive change. Opportunities for student advocacy can occur on campus, within the school district, or within the local, state, and federal political arenas.

Confidentiality

Maintaining Student Confidentiality

A school leader must maintain student confidentiality according to the Family Educational Rights and Privacy Act (FERPA). This involves keeping student information and records confidential. However, when advocating for students, the school leader may be informed of student information by other staff members, parents, or the students themselves that should also be kept confidential. Keeping the students' confidentiality means not sharing private information with outside parties unnecessarily. This fosters trust between the school leader and the student or other stakeholders. Establishing this trust helps to create a school culture in which students and their families are willing to share sensitive information with the school staff to help advocate for a student. For example, a parent may inform the school leader that the family has recently become homeless. Certain documents must be completed and certain staff need to be informed of this information to advocate for the homeless student, but the school leader must ensure that the sensitive information remains as private as possible. There are circumstances in which the student's confidentiality may need to be breached, but the school leader should make an effort to maintain that confidentiality.

Situations in Which Student Confidentiality Must Be Breached

A school leader and other school staff must do their best to maintain the confidence of students, but under some circumstances a student's confidentiality must be breached. If students confide in a staff member that they are being harmed, pose harm to themselves, or pose harm to others, school staff members have the responsibility to act on that information for the protection of those students or others. For example, a student may confide in a teacher that he or she is contemplating suicide. The teacher would then break the student's confidentiality and inform the school leader of the student's intentions. The teacher and the school leader would then contact the student's parents and the proper authorities to obtain immediate help for the student. Other examples that warrant a breach in student confidentiality include information related to child abuse or neglect or threats of violence to others.

Motivating Students

Intrinsic Motivation

Intrinsic motivation is motivation that comes from within. It is a person's own drive to succeed or to accomplish a goal. For students, this intrinsic motivation may be the result of education and career goals, family expectations, social influences, and more. Intrinsic motivation may drive students to meet or exceed academic performance expectations, participate in and excel in extracurricular activities, or choose certain education and career pathways. Intrinsic motivation is affected very little by outside influences because the drive comes from within. For example, a high school student may desire to become a writer and consequently excels in English Language Arts classes. This student may have an English Language Arts teacher that he or she does not get along with, but because the drive to become a writer is intrinsic, the student may still work hard and perform well in that class. Intrinsic motivation is considered more effective than extrinsic motivation. Students who excel in school, especially in the face of obstacles and challenges, are often intrinsically motivated.

Extrinsic Motivation

Extrinsic motivation is motivation that comes from an outside source, such as another person, and is in the form of a reward. The reward can be tangible, such as money, prizes, or gifts, or it can be intangible, such as an experience, recognition, or approval. Teachers and other staff often use extrinsic motivation to encourage students to perform at a certain level or behave in a certain way. For example, a teacher may tell her third-grade class that all students who complete their homework will receive stickers. The students will be motivated to complete their homework and earn stickers. Extrinsic motivation can be effective with students, especially when they are lacking intrinsic motivation. However, extrinsic motivation is considered less effective than intrinsic motivation because in the absence of the reward, motivation significantly decreases. Additionally, if the reward loses its appeal, motivation will decrease. For example, if the third-grade teacher were to stop offering stickers for homework, the number of completed homework assignments might decline. Similarly, students may be less excited about receiving stickers for homework near the end of the school year, resulting in fewer completed homework assignments.

Motivating Students

School staff can create systems of rewards to motivate students to engage in the academic program, perform at higher levels, and behave in an acceptable manner. Rewards can be given for individual and collective behaviors. Some schools have used point systems or merit systems to reward and motivate students. Students can redeem points for prizes, participation in field trips, or participation in other school activities. Some schools use stickers, tickets, or other means of reinforcing positive student behaviors, which can be redeemed as well. For example, a student may earn a ticket for participating in class discussion, which can be redeemed for a prize. This reward would encourage the student to increase participation in class discussion. Students may also be motivated by public recognition, such as receiving an award at an awards ceremony, being identified on the school website or a classroom bulletin board, or having their names announced during school announcements. Students are motivated when rewards systems are clear, fair, and consistent and when expectations are clearly outlined.

Aspects of the School That Can Demotivate Students

Perceived negative aspects of the school can decrease student motivation, causing them to disengage in the school program. If a student perceives school as unsafe, he or she may have poor school attendance or arrive late to school. If a student perceives the teacher to be unfair or ineffective, the student may not desire to perform well in that class, resulting in poor grades and possibly behavioral problems. When students perceive school rules or policies as unfair or unequitable, they may be discouraged from abiding by those policies or engaging in the programs that the policies or procedures apply to. For example, a student may desire to audition for a role in the school play. However, the student views the audition process as unfair and believes that certain students will be chosen for the roles regardless of who auditions. Consequently, that student will choose not to audition for the play or engage in the theater program. School leaders must identify aspects of the school and school program that may demotivate students and remedy these where possible.

Transparent Decision-Making Based on Data

Transparent Decision-Making

Transparent decision-making is the act of making sure that the process, logic, and rationale used to make a decision are clear and open to others. When decision-making is transparent, any critical information used to inform that decision is also readily available to others for review. This transparency allows others to understand how the decision was made. For example, if a school leader were to make a decide whether to eliminate the art program, a transparent decision-making process would allow stakeholders and team members to observe and understand how the school leader makes the decision. The process may start with publicly making known that the decision needed to be made. Then, data relating to the art program would be provided, including data related to any other programming that may be compared to the art program. Additional rationale could be documented, such as evaluating the position of the art program in relation to the school vision and goals. Based on this relevant information, observers of the decision-making process would be able to understand and even predict the decision that the leader would make.

Using Data to Support Transparent Decision-Making

Data is essential to offering transparency in decision-making. Data is objective, which makes it less refutable. Stakeholders may question or contest a school leader's decisions in some cases, but are less likely to question or contest the data influencing those decisions. Data that is shared may include financial data, student performance data, or data related to school demographics such as enrollment, attendance, or discipline. When data is shared with stakeholders, it is easier for them to understand the basis and determining factors for decisions. For example, if a school leader decides to eliminate a school program based on poor student participation, the school leader can be transparent and provide the attendance and participation data for that program to the stakeholders. As a result, the stakeholders will understand that the decision is based on objective data. Additionally, basing decisions on data will encourage the school leader to make sound decisions based on concrete data whenever possible because the school leader will be aware that the decision-making process will be observed by stakeholders.

Most Effective Data in Supporting Transparent Decision-Making

Staff

Providing data is an essential component of transparency in decision-making. The school leader can share data such as school performance data and individual student data to demonstrate how a decision was made. Teachers and staff understand this data and, as employees working directly with students, are able to look at student data. This data can help them understand why decisions are made about certain curricular programs, school discipline procedures, and other aspects of the school program. Also, the school leader can use data to support conversations with staff regarding individual performance, which can lead to decision-making. For example, a school leader may determine that a third-grade reading teacher should be reassigned to a fourth-grade classroom. The leader can use student performance data and the teacher's performance evaluation data to explain the decision to the teacher. A school leader should always protect the confidentiality of students and personnel when applicable.

Community Stakeholders

Providing data is an essential component of transparency in decision making. When being transparent with stakeholders, the school leader must be careful to protect the confidentiality of school, student, and personnel data. As a result, the school leader should be selective about the data that is shared with stakeholders and the manner in which it is shared. Data that is already public and is used to make a decision can be helpful when sharing data with stakeholders. The school leader should be prepared to explain the data, the measures used to obtain it, and its implications. Although the school leader cannot share individual student and staff data, the school leader can share aggregates of the data. For example, the school leader may provide data of third-grade student performance on a recent benchmark assessment. Data that is shared with stakeholders should be clear, easy to understand, and purposeful so that it adds to the transparency of the decision-making process.

Allowing for Feedback

Importance of Gathering Feedback

Feedback is the process of gathering information from an outside source to evaluate or correct a particular course of action. A school leader should seek feedback to ensure that he or she is on the correct path when making decisions. Without feedback, a school leader may proceed with a course of action, only to realize later that it was a mistake. For example, a leader may decide to host parent meetings on Wednesday evenings. After hosting the first meeting with poor turnout, the leader may find that many families in the community attend church on Wednesday evenings. Had the leader gathered feedback, a different time might have been chosen. Gathering feedback can help the school leader make corrections or alter a course in a timely manner. Additionally, gathering feedback from stakeholders demonstrates that the school leader is humble and receptive to feedback. Perceived humility in the leader can help in team building and relationship building with the staff and the community. Gathering feedback also increases buy-in from those providing the feedback, such as members of the leadership team, key community members, or school district office personnel.

Gathering Feedback

A school leader can gather feedback from stakeholders in various ways to aid in their decision-making. A primary way of gathering feedback is presenting ideas and plans to the campus leadership team. The leadership team may include assistant principals, deans, or other leaders on campus. This team is effective in providing feedback because they know the campus, students, and community well and have demonstrated leadership skills and thinking. For example, the leadership team may provide feedback on a lunch schedule based on their experiences from lunch duty in the cafeteria. Also, supervising district personnel are often available to provide feedback to the school leader, especially in confidential matters. The school leader can also solicit feedback from students, parents, and community members. This type of feedback can help the school leader see situations and potential decisions from other perspectives. For example, a student may provide feedback that the proposed after school program does not interest the student body. Also, gathering and implementing feedback from stakeholders can increase stakeholder buy-in and support of the school's vision and goals.

Responding to Negative Feedback

When a leader solicits feedback from students, staff, or stakeholders, it is possible that the feedback may be negative. The negative feedback may be in relation to aspects of the school program or in relation to the leader. When a leader receives feedback, he or she must avoid an immediate emotional response to the feedback. First the leader must determine whether the feedback has validity. Persons providing feedback can sometimes speak out of anger or frustration and deliver the feedback in a harsh way. However, delivery of the feedback does not necessarily determine whether the feedback is valid. Consequently, the leader must reflect upon his or her practice and identify whether the feedback identifies an area of improvement for the leader or the school program. If so, the leader must acknowledge this weak area and take steps to improve it. When improvements have been made, if possible, the leader should seek feedback once again to determine if the concerns of the stakeholders have been addressed.

Responding to Positive Feedback

Positive feedback from stakeholders can be encouraging for the school leader. Sometimes this feedback is solicited and other times it is volunteered. Positive feedback can be used for reflection and improvement. First, the leader needs to determine the validity of the feedback. Some people may feel the need to offer flattery or unsubstantiated positive feedback in an effort to favorably position themselves. Therefore, a leader must not assume that his or her performance or the school's performance is favorable because one or two persons offered a compliment. Next, the leader must not become overconfident in the area that has received positive feedback. Instead, the feedback should encourage the leader to continue the actions that led to the favorable outcome to continue to achieve good results. Positive feedback can also be shared with other staff so they can be assured that they are performing well in the identified area.

Honest Self-Reflection

Conducting Honest Self-Reflection

Honest self-reflection is a component of growth and efficacy as a school leader. A school leader should set aside time to reflect on personal performance as a leader, based on identified leadership expectations and standards. There are many models of leadership that the school leader can use for comparison, but most school districts select or develop a tool for leadership evaluation. These evaluation tools include the expectations for leadership skills, performance, and behaviors. School leaders can use the tools to identify their own strengths and weaknesses. Also, any time a leader is reading professional materials such as books or articles related to leadership, it is an opportunity to reflect on how he or she measures against the skills identified in the resource. Often, stakeholders such as parents or community members offer criticisms of the leader. The school leader should reflect upon the validity of those criticisms to determine areas for improvement. For example, during a parent conference, a parent may complain that the leader is a poor communicator. Even though the parent may have made the statement in a moment of frustration or anger, the school leader should take the opportunity to reflect upon his or her communication skills and how those skills were used in that situation.

Addressing Weaknesses Revealed Through Self-Reflection

Once a leader has identified weaknesses through self-reflection, he or she can take several steps to address them. First, the school leader can read books, articles, and other resources related to the areas of weakness. For example, if the school leader has difficulty with time management, he or she can identify resources that can help to cultivate better time management skills. A leader can also participate in training or professional development related to the identified areas of weakness. A variety of professional organizations provide workshops and training related to various leadership competencies. The leader can also seek assistance from a supervisor or other district staff person. A supervisor can offer suggestions or guidance for improvement in a deficient area. Additionally, the school leader can obtain mentors and coaches outside of the school organization that can provide objective skill building in the school leader's deficit areas. Mentors may be retired principals or other types of leaders who are in the school leader's network and are willing to share their expertise. Mentors do not typically require payment. In contrast, coaches are often hired to help with targeted skill-building and professional growth.

Effect of Leader's Self-Reflection on the Leadership Team

A leader's self-reflection can affect the leadership team in a number of ways. First, it sets an example as a school leader that self-reflection should be a part of leadership practice. This also demonstrates to the leadership team that the leader is aware that he or she is not perfect and is making efforts to address identified weaknesses. The leadership team should be comprised of people who help to compensate for the leader's weaknesses. Therefore, when a leader identifies his or her weaknesses, this can lead to adjustment of the leadership team. For example, if the leader determines that his or her leadership in math and science is weak, the leader may identify a person who is strong in math and science to be a part of the leadership team. Additionally, a leader's self-reflection can lead to shifting roles and responsibilities on the leadership team and reflection about the strengths and weaknesses of the entire team.

Effect of Leader's Self-Reflection on Stakeholders

A leader's self-reflection can affect how he or she is perceived by stakeholders as well as the leader's relationship with stakeholders. When stakeholders observe the leader committing to self-improvement and making changes, they may conclude that the leader is humble and willing to improve the practice and the operation of the school. This can build hope and trust among stakeholders. For example, the leader may communicate to stakeholders that he or she is working on improving communication skills and is committed to doing a better job of returning phone calls and responding to emails. Similarly, engagement in self-reflection and self-improvement demonstrates that the leader is responsive to feedback. It is difficult to engage with a leader who believes that he or she knows everything, does not need feedback, and cannot receive criticism. In contrast, a leader who reflects and improves can encourage stakeholders to engage with the leader and the school and relationships can be built between the leader and stakeholders.

Professional Learning and Growth Leadership

Recruiting and Evaluating Staff Members

Recruiting Teachers and Other Staff Members

A leader should be strategic in recruiting new teachers and staff members. To determine whether candidates will be a good fit on the campus, the leader should examine them in relation to the school culture, vision, and goals. A leader should first use the school culture as criteria for recruitment. For example, if the school culture is one of innovation and creativity, the leader will want to recruit candidates who have demonstrated creativity in the past and are comfortable taking the risks necessary to try new things. Also, the leader will want to recruit candidates with the necessary skills to aid in implementing the school vision and goals. For example, if the school vision is to become an exemplary campus in the integration of technology into the learning process, the leader should recruit candidates who are skilled with technology and are comfortable utilizing it. Using such criteria when recruiting teachers and other candidates will ensure that they will be a good fit on campus and contribute to the school's success.

Including Other Team Members in the Recruitment Process

Including other team members in the recruitment process is beneficial for several reasons. First, having more than one person participating in this process reduces the potential for demonstrating bias during the recruitment and hiring process. Other team members may notice aspects of potential candidates that the leader missed, which can help to provide a well-rounded view of each candidate. Also, other team members may have different perspectives regarding the needs and dynamics of the campus, which can help to determine whether potential candidates are a good fit for open positions. Lastly, staff morale and campus culture can benefit from allowing team members to participate in the process of selecting their future coworkers. Some schools allow students to participate in the recruitment and selection process of teaching candidates because they are the ones who will ultimately be affected.

Evaluating Staff Members

For a campus to reach its goals and achieve its vision, all staff members must perform to expectations. It is essential that staff members be evaluated to ensure that all are performing to expectations. Evaluations of staff members provide an opportunity for leaders to identify areas of strength and weakness among the staff and to provide constructive feedback to staff members so that they can grow professionally. Leaders can use these evaluations to determine what additional support and resources are needed to support or improve the staff member performance. For example, a leader may discover through evaluation that the science department demonstrates deficiencies in providing hands-on instruction to students. The leader can then identify professional development and coaching to assist the science teachers in improving this area. Evaluations are also used to determine whether staff members will have continued employment on campus. Staff members who consistently perform below expectations may have to be removed from their position and assigned to a different position or campus.

Evaluating Teachers

State law requires that teachers be evaluated with a standardized evaluation system. The state may recommend a certain teacher evaluation system, but school districts can often choose which system to implement. Whether the school district adopts the recommended evaluation tool or develops its own, the standards for evaluation must meet or exceed the expectations outlined by the state. For teachers to be evaluated, the evaluators (usually campus administrators such as principals and assistant principals) must be trained in using the tool. Additionally, teachers must be trained on the tool that will be used to evaluate them. Evaluation often includes regular observations by the evaluator, collection of artifacts or data related to their practice, and conferences with the evaluator to discuss feedback. Teacher evaluation is usually based on performance in relation to the standards outlined in the evaluation tool, as well as growth or progress. Teacher performance standards are often related to instructional practice and strategies, professionalism, growth and professional development, and student performance. The evaluation process occurs throughout the school year and teachers receive a final evaluation rating at the conclusion of the school year.

Observe Staff Performance in Varied Scenarios

Observing Staff Performance

Leaders should use as many opportunities as possible to observe staff performance so they will have a well-rounded view of the performance. The opportunities may include various days of the week or times of day, as well as varied circumstances. Teachers can be observed while engaging in their instructional practice in the classroom. They can also be observed while they are engaged in collaboration as they participate in professional learning communities. Additionally, teachers can be observed while they are fulfilling duty assignments such as arrival, dismissal, cafeteria, or hall duty. Other staff members can also be observed at different times, whether performing normal duties or engaging in special events such as community events, student events, or district events. A leader should be intentional and deliberate about seeking out different opportunities to observe staff at a variety of times, in a variety of circumstances, to obtain a fair and holistic view of staff performance.

Observing Staff in a Variety of Scenarios at Different Times

It is important to observe staff in a variety of scenarios and at different times to get an accurate impression of staff performance. If a leader observes a staff member infrequently or always at the same time, this may lead to an inaccurate perception of that person's performance. For teachers, class dynamics may vary throughout the day. When a leader does not vary the time of day for observing a teacher, he or she will not know how that teacher responds to varied classroom dynamics or how instruction is practiced in all of the assigned courses. For example, a teacher may have a small class in the afternoon with fewer challenges than other classes. If a leader observes the teacher only during that class, he or she may not see all of the instructional and classroom management skills that the teacher demonstrates throughout the school day. If a leader consistently observes a teacher at the same time, it can also lead to predictability. A staff person could prepare for observation, so that it is not an authentic reflection of that person's regular work performance.

Improving Staff Performance

Conducting observations can help to improve staff performance by providing opportunity for feedback and growth. Observations allow a leader to see a staff member in action. When a leader observes a teacher or other staff member, he or she will note strengths and weaknesses in that employee's performance in relation to campus and district expectations. The leader can specifically reference what was observed as evidence of those strengths and weaknesses. This data will then help the leader to provide feedback regarding performance. The leader can also provide suggestions for improvement or give access to professional development and resources that will help the staff member to improve. Observations can also illustrate staff members' strengths so that they can build on them and continue to grow in those areas. Feedback and recommendations can also be used immediately to improve performance.

Calibration Among Staff Evaluators

One campus may include multiple people who evaluate the performance of teachers and staff. The process of calibration is the training of all evaluators to maintain and look for the same standards of performance. When a team is not calibrated, different evaluators may have different perceptions of excellence, which can lead to confusion and inconsistency in staff performance. To calibrate staff evaluators, the team of evaluators should observe a staff person together at the same time. They each conduct an observation as if they were conducting it alone. After the observation is complete, the team of evaluators meets to discuss what they observed and how they would evaluate the staff person. The leader helps the team identify where their evaluations are aligned or misaligned in regard to the performance expectations. For example, a leader may believe that the observed teacher did a poor job implementing collaborative learning, while another evaluator believes that the teacher implemented collaborative learning in an acceptable manner. The leader would then refer to the performance standards and discuss the observed evidence to reach a consensus. This process would be repeated until all evaluators are able to assess staff members in like manner.

Develops Processes to Support Teachers' Growth

Supporting Teachers' Growth with Evaluations

Teacher evaluations support their growth because evaluations help to identify areas of needed improvement and hold teachers accountable for addressing those areas. Evaluations are based on a set of performance standards and will reveal if a teacher is not adequately meeting any of those standards. A teacher who needs to improve will know exactly where to focus improvement efforts, based on the evaluation results. The evaluation will also help the leader know how to best support the teacher in growing professionally. Additionally, evaluations hold teachers accountable for improving their practice. The accountability comes from the process of conducting evaluations, including timelines and deadlines, self-reflection, and conversations with the evaluator regarding areas of growth. When professional growth or efforts to achieve growth are not observed in the teacher, the teacher is at risk for receiving a negative evaluation at the end of the school year. A negative evaluation could result in outcomes such as probation or termination. The process of evaluating teachers ensures that they are growing professionally to become the best teachers they can be.

Selecting Professional Development for Staff Members

A leader needs to be deliberate in selecting professional development for staff members so that it is purposeful in helping staff achieve the campus goals and vision. One strategy a leader can use includes analyzing how the professional development aligns with the campus vision and goals. For example, if the campus goal is to increase reading performance, then selecting a professional development session on implementing effective reading instructional practices would be appropriate. Another strategy that a leader can use to select professional development is to identify weak areas of staff based on observations and evaluations. A leader may observe that several teachers are having difficulty implementing effective classroom management strategies, so that leader may seek out professional development that addresses classroom management. Also, a leader must ensure that staff members participate in professional development that is mandated by the district or the state, such as something related to special populations of students or law and policy.

Supporting Teachers' Growth with Coaching

A coach is a professional who helps a teacher to develop the skills necessary to work effectively. A coach is a staff person who does not supervise or evaluate the person being coached. This helps to foster a relationship of trust between the coach and the teacher. A coach will identify a teacher's areas of strengths and weakness based on a predetermined rubric or set of expectations. Then the coach will provide one-on-one support to help the teacher improve targeted areas. The coach may provide books and resources or recommend professional development sessions. The coach may also model effective teaching, observe the teacher in practice to provide real-time feedback, assist in the lesson planning process, and guide the teacher in self-reflection and critical analysis processes. A coach provides individualized, targeted support to teachers, which helps them to grow, usually in a shorter period of time than other forms of professional development support.

Utilizing High-Performing Teachers to Support the Growth of Other Teachers

High-performing teachers on campus can support the growth of other teachers by becoming leaders, serving as models, and coaching. High-performing teachers may exceed performance expectations in many areas or only a few, but their strengths can be leveraged to benefit the other teachers on campus. A leader may utilize high-performing teachers as leaders on campus in several ways. These teachers may be promoted to lead departments or be tasked with leading collaborative meetings, such as professional learning communities. Leaders may also direct these teachers to lead on-campus professional development sessions relating to their areas of strength. These teachers can also serve as models to the other teachers. Teachers who need to improve in certain areas may be asked to observe a high-performing teacher to see how a particular skill or strategy is implemented in the classroom. A high-performing teacher can also have a coaching role for other teachers to provide one-one-one support in certain performance areas.

Recommends Appropriate Teaching and Learning Practices

Importance of the Principal as an Instructional Leader

The principal should act as the instructional leader on campus. This is important because it helps the leader to focus on instruction on campus, helps to support teachers, and establishes credibility with the faculty. When a principal is an instructional leader, instruction is prioritized. This impacts all school operations, including scheduling, alignment of resources, and support. Also, instructional leaders are able to support teachers in improving their skills related to teaching and learning. A principal who is experienced in and familiar with instruction will be a better evaluator of instruction and can offer expertise in improving instructional practice. Also, acting as an instructional leader gives validity to the principal's feedback relating to instruction. Teachers will be more receptive to feedback and advice regarding their instructional practice if the leader has demonstrated that he or she prioritizes instruction and has knowledge and expertise in that area. The principal should be prepared and willing to take the lead instructionally on campus in a variety of forms, such as providing feedback, demonstrating or modeling expectations, and collaborating and problem-solving with teaching staff.

Importance of the School Leader's Participation in Professional Development

A principal should participate in professional development for his or her own growth and development and to demonstrate solidarity with staff members. When possible, a leader should participate in professional development with the staff so that he or she can learn as well. When the leader participates in the professional development, this helps to identify the actions and behaviors he or she can expect from staff that also participate in the session. For example, if teachers participated in a professional development session regarding collaborative learning strategies, the leader would need to know what effective implementation of those strategies would look like in the classroom and how to support teachers as they implement them. Also, when the leader participates in professional development with staff, this demonstrates to the team that the leader values the opportunity for professional development and views it as a priority. This will increase buy-in from the staff and help them to be more receptive of the information and training that they receive at the professional development session.

Collaborative Teaching and Learning

Collaborative teaching involves two or more teachers engaging in instruction together. Collaborative teaching can take many forms, such as team teaching, co-teaching, and others. For example, one teacher may act as a lead teacher and present instruction to students while the other teacher acts as a support, helping to manage student behavior and reinforce concepts with struggling students. In another model, a teacher may present new instruction to students while another teacher in the room provides remedial or intervention instruction to a small group of students. Other team teaching models involve students being divided into groups and receiving new instruction from a teacher within their groups. In a team teaching model in which both teachers act as lead teachers, there are often student rotations or instructional stations involved. Collaborative teaching requires co-planning on the part of the team teachers and a good working relationship between them. Collaborative teaching allows for more flexibility within the classroom and exposes students to differentiated instruction and a variety of teaching styles.

Structure of Professional Learning Communities

Professional learning communities can be structured in a variety of ways to support collaboration among educators on campus. Most often, these professional learning communities are organized in a way that allows staff with shared roles or responsibilities to collaborate together under the leadership of one person who is designated to lead the community and is often trained to do so. For example, a professional learning community structured by grade level may consist of all eighth-grade teachers. In contrast, a community structured by content area may consist of all math teachers on campus. The campus leader may determine which structure best meets the needs of the teachers and students. Professional learning communities are usually goal-driven, which encourages participants to collaborate in order to achieve the established goals. Professional learning communities are often guided by the following questions: What do we want students to learn? How do we know if they learned it? What do we do if they did not learn it? What do we do if they did learn it? While participation in professional learning communities may be voluntary on some campuses, for many schools it is mandatory for teachers to participate.

Purpose of Professional Learning Communities

The purpose of professional learning communities, also referred to as PLCs, is to improve the educational performance and achievement of students through educator collaboration. PLCs are structured ways to facilitate sharing knowledge and improving skills among educators through data analysis, action research, exchange of expertise, and professional dialogue. In PLCs, teachers may discuss their practice and seek ways to improve. For example, teachers participating in a PLC may share lesson plans with committee members for feedback. Teachers may also share student work with committee members to calibrate grading practices or solicit ways to improve the quality of students' work. For example, a teacher may present a sample of student writing to committee members to get feedback on suggested focus areas for subsequent instruction. Teachers may also discuss student performance data in PLCs. This data may include summative assessment within the classroom or formative assessment, such as benchmark data or standardized testing data. Teachers may also use PLCs to discuss professional literature.

Benefits of Collaborative Teaching and Learning

There are many benefits of collaborative teaching and learning. When teachers collaborate, they are able to share ideas. This fosters innovation and growth on campus. Collaboration also helps to solve problems more quickly. When a teacher has an issue, other teachers can provide resources, suggestions, or advice to help address the issue so the teacher does not have to research solutions independently and attempt to solve the problem through trial and error. For example, if a teacher has difficulty reaching a particular student, collaborating with other teachers who have that student in class and have been successful can help to identify ways that the teacher can reach the student. Also, collaboration among teachers builds community and fortifies the school culture. When teachers work and plan together, they build relationships with one another that can foster feelings of belonging and support. Teachers who are collaborative know that they can celebrate successes with their team members and that if they have a problem or challenge, they have a team of supporters. When teachers have these types of relationships and feel supported, it is easier to retain them in the classroom and encourage them to grow professionally.

Supporting Collaborative Teaching and Learning on Campus

A school leader is instrumental in ensuring that teachers are able to collaborate on campus. First, the school leader must plan a school schedule that allows for collaboration. This could mean that there are designated times for professional learning communities or that teachers who need to plan together have planning periods scheduled at the same time. For example, if the school leader expects all teachers in a certain grade level to collaborate, then the instructional schedule must accommodate a shared planning time for those teachers. The school leader also needs to train staff how to participate in a collaborative learning environment in line with the campus vision and goals. This requires the leader to set clear expectations for the operation and outcomes of collaborative planning, such as those outlined in professional learning communities. Also, the leader must designate teachers or leadership team members to lead collaborative planning so that there is organization and accountability. Finally, the leader can support collaborative teaching and learning by participating in collaborative meetings when possible and modeling collaboration in other areas.

Collaborative Learning

Collaborative learning is an instructional strategy in which students are organized into groups for learning. These learning groups allow students to support each other and dialogue about the instruction and content. Collaborative learning reinforces listening and speaking skills in addition to the presented content. Teachers may employ several different strategies to organize students into collaborative groups. These include ability grouping (or homogenous grouping), heterogeneous grouping, and flexible grouping. In homogenous grouping, a teacher may organize students into groups based on proficiency with a certain skill so that targeted support and activities can be provided to groups based on their collective need. In heterogeneous grouping, students with different strengths or skills may be grouped together to balance out the group's deficits. Students may remain in these designated groups for a certain period of time, such as a grading period. Flexible groups are dynamic and take on different forms based on the instructional goals set by the teacher. These groups may have different sizes and composition based on needs.

Appropriating Resources for Effective Instruction

Supporting Instruction Through Appropriation of Physical Resources

Effective instruction requires appropriate physical resources. The leader can support instruction on campus by providing adequate physical resources for instructional staff. Physical resources include all of the tangible items needed to deliver instruction, such as furniture, books, and supplies. For example, classroom spaces must be able to accommodate teachers and learners, so there must be an adequate number of desks or tables and chairs, as well as physical square footage of the instructional space. Also, teachers need access to instructional supplies and appropriate technology for instruction. Other physical resources include curriculum, textbooks, computer labs, and other instructional resources. Leaders can identify necessary physical resources based on the school's vision and goals. For example, if the campus is striving to excel in STEM instruction, the leader needs to equip the school with science materials, computers, and other physical resources required for effective STEM instruction. Also, the leader may seek feedback from instructional staff regarding the necessary resources to be effective in the classroom. For example, a teacher may need additional bookshelves to accommodate leveled books within the classroom.

Supporting Instruction Through the Appropriation of Human Resources

Effective instruction requires the appropriate staff in place to deliver and support the instructional program. Human resources that are part of the instructional program include teachers, librarians, aides, and many others. A leader must ensure that the right number of people with the appropriate skills and qualifications are placed in the appropriate instructional positions. For example, it is the leader's responsibility to ensure that all classes are assigned a highly-qualified teacher for the start of the school year. This may mean that the leader actively recruits and screens teaching candidates to have a fully-staffed campus throughout the school year. Additionally, a leader must respond to needs for additional staffing or changes in staffing throughout the school year. For example, if students demonstrate deficits in math, the leader may identify math tutors to provide additional instruction. Also, a leader may notice that students with special needs require more support within the classroom and can implement a co-teaching model to support instruction. The leader can also seek feedback from staff to determine where additional instructional staff may be needed or where staff changes need to be made.

Importance of Resources for Effective Instruction

A leader must ensure that the appropriate resources are provided to instructional staff in order to support effective instruction on campus. A lack of resources on campus can make it difficult for teachers to teach and for students to learn. For example, if a teacher is assigned 22 students in her classroom, but there are only 20 desks, the teacher will have difficulty arranging her classroom in a way that is conducive to learning. Also, if a classroom does not have a highly-qualified teacher assigned to it, students will lose out on quality instructional time. In contrast, when teachers and other instructional staff are provided with the physical and human resources needed for effective instruction, both they and the students benefit. For example, if the school's vision is to cultivate reading skills in students, teachers would benefit from books, bookshelves, online reading programs, a library, and a librarian in order to achieve that vision. As a leader may not be able to provide all of the desired resources for instructional staff, he or she must decide which resources can be provided based on the school budget.

Overcoming Budget Challenges When Providing Instructional Resources to Teachers

At times, the school budget will not be sufficient to provide the desired instructional resources for teachers. In these instances, a school leader may need to seek additional ways to provide these resources. One way to overcome this challenge is to seek funding from outside the school. This may mean applying for grants or seeking donations from various businesses and organizations. The funds acquired can be used to purchase the desired resources. An additional strategy is to ask the manufacturers to donate the resources to the school. The school may volunteer to be a pilot school for the implementation of the resources. Also, parent organizations can conduct fundraisers to supplement the school budget and secure the needed resources. For example, the PTO may conduct a fundraiser to purchase supplies for the art program. The school leader should also determine whether the next school year's budget should accommodate the resources for the subsequent school year.

Time Management

Using Planning Time to Support Effective Instruction

Teachers have planning time scheduled into their instructional day. This planning time is determined when the master class schedule is designed for the campus, so leaders must consider in advance how much time is allotted to teachers for planning. A leader should encourage teachers to use this time to support effective instruction. For example, teachers can assess the quality of student work, prepare feedback for students, and determine which skills or content may need to be retaught. Planning time can be used to examine resources and determine how they can be incorporated into instruction or to identify differentiated instructional strategies for reaching diverse learners. Teachers may also choose to collaborate with other teachers in the planning and delivery of lessons. Leaders should ensure that teachers have adequate planning time and access to resources to support their efforts during planning time. Additionally, leaders should be considerate of teachers' planning time by avoiding scheduling meetings, conferences, duty, or other assignments during this time whenever possible.

Impact of Time Management on Instruction

Instruction on a school campus is delivered according to a strict schedule. Specific times are allotted for various aspects of the instructional program. A school leader's ability to manage his or her own time as well as to occupy the time of other campus staff can affect instruction. For example, the leader's timeliness in approving decisions relating to instruction can impact the timeline of projects. The timeframe in which the school leader obtains resources for the instructional program can also impact instruction. For example, if the campus would like to integrate technology into the curriculum, the leader's ability to secure computers for the students and teachers affects when instruction could begin. Additionally, the leader's daily decision-making regarding use of time can impact instruction, such as scheduling of meetings, school assemblies and activities, and conferences with staff. The leader must manage his or her time in planning, decision-making, and other duties throughout the school day to support the instructional program.

Preserving Instructional Time

Preserving instructional time means reducing the number of distractions and interruptions to the instructional program, specifically the time students spend in the classroom. Interruptions to instructional time may include announcements, school assemblies, meetings, or any other activities or events that distract from the instructional routine. For example, a campus leader may desire to host a school-wide event such as a pep rally during the school day. The leader would need to consider the impact on the instructional day from hosting such an event. He or she may decide to adjust the day's schedule by taking a few minutes from each class, rather than having students miss a large portion of instructional time from one class, to accommodate the event at the end of the day. A leader may also decide that a pep rally does not warrant the interruption of instructional time and instead may postpone the event. Leaders who preserve instructional time use school-wide public announcements sparingly, adjust schedules for school assemblies to reduce the impact on instructional time, and try to schedule other meetings and events outside of the instructional day when possible.

Allocating Funds and Budgeting

How School Funding Is Calculated

School funding comes from a variety of sources. The federal government provides some funding. This is not usually substantial and may fluctuate due to changing budget decisions at the federal level. The state governments also provide funding to schools based on income and/or sales taxes.

The majority of school funding is gained from property taxes within the school district. Both residences and commercial properties are taxed and a portion of those taxes are allocated to school districts. Schools generally receive an allotment of funds on a per-pupil basis. The per-pupil allotment differs by school district but may average about $10,000 per pupil. However, certain programs warrant extra funds on top of this allotment, such as special education programs and technology programs. Schools and school districts often seek grants and donations from foundations to supplement their budget.

Centralized Budgeting and Decentralized Budgeting

Centralized and decentralized budgeting refers to the locus of control for budgeting decisions within a school district. In a centralized school district, all budgetary decision-making is conducted by district leaders within the district office. Principals and the campuses they lead have little to no budgetary authority in a centralized district. When a district is centralized, principals must follow strict guidelines as to what can be purchased and when. The benefit of a centralized budgeting process is that budgeting decisions are controlled and quality and efficiency can be easily monitored. However, this type of system can prevent staff buy-in and cause school leaders to feel they do not have the authority to make the changes necessary for their school to be successful. In contrast, in a decentralized district, principals have authority to make budgetary and purchasing decisions. This allows principals to determine which resources meet the needs of each individual campus and gives them the latitude and flexibility to address campus needs. The benefit of a decentralized budgeting process is the flexibility and increased buy-in of leaders. However, this type of system can be more difficult to monitor and cause more instances of mismanagement of funds.

Factors to Consider When Allocating Funds

A leader should consider multiple factors when allocating funds. First, the leader should refer to the school's vision. The allocation of funds should align with that vision. Similarly, the leader should align the allocation of funds to the school's goals. It is likely that the goals that are set for the school require funds and resources to accomplish them, so these funds should be allocated first. A leader should also consider whether funds are recurring or one-time funds. When a school receives funds that will not be renewed, a school leader must ensure that whatever is completed with those funds is sustainable for the future once those funds are gone. The school leader must also evaluate the school program and organizational structure to ensure that sufficient funds are allocated to the successful and efficient operation of the school program.

Factors That Affect a School's Budget Each Year

A school's budget is not fixed but can vary from year to year based on a variety of factors. Funding from the federal and state government can fluctuate and impact campus budgeting. In some years, the government provides one-time funding that cannot be expected in subsequent years, which causes fluctuations. Additionally, the government can change allocations of funding for specific programs. For example, allocation of funding for Career and Technology Education may be altered, so even though the number of students participating in the program does not change, the received funds do. Local property taxes may change in a school district, affecting the money allocated to schools. Additional factors include changes in student enrollment, changes in school programming, and other factors. Each year, a school leader must evaluate the proposed budget for the school year and make decisions based on each year's budgetary allocations.

Strategies for Recruiting Highly Qualified Personnel

Highly Qualified

The term "highly qualified" is used to describe the minimum qualifications of a teacher according to the No Child Left Behind Act, enacted in 2001. To meet staffing expectations, a leader has the responsibility of ensuring that teachers are highly qualified. This means that the teacher must hold a bachelor's degree and either have full state licensure/certification or demonstrate knowledge of the subject that he or she will teach. Based on this definition, states have enacted various procedures that enable teachers to demonstrate their content area knowledge, such as testing. A teacher may be highly qualified in one subject area and not in another. For example, a teacher may be deemed highly qualified to teach chemistry due to holding a bachelor's degree in science and being state certified in chemistry, but that same teacher would not be highly qualified to teach biology. Having highly qualified staff on campus ensures that teachers are knowledgeable in their assigned content areas and capable of teaching the content to students.

Recruiting Highly Qualified Personnel

Leaders can employ several strategies to recruit highly qualified personnel. Leaders can participate in recruitment fairs. These are often hosted by the school district or by community organizations. Leaders can follow up with persons from the event for interviews or may even conduct screening interviews at these fairs. Also, leaders can contact teacher preparation programs for referrals of recently certified teachers. These entities have lists of recent graduates along with their areas of specialization. However, these lists include persons with limited or no teaching experience. It can also be helpful to post advertisements on traditional recruitment sites. Some sites specialize in recruiting for education. Finally, leaders can use word of mouth advertising to recruit highly qualified personnel. Teachers and staff on campus may have colleagues in other locations who would like to work at a new school. For example, a person may want to work at a school that is closer to home or teach a different grade level.

Importance of Being Fully Staffed at the Outset of the School Year

If a school leader has numerous teaching vacancies, it can be difficult to have all staff in place at the outset of the school year. However, the beginning of the school year is a critical time that can impact the success of the entire school year, so a leader should strive to have 100% of staff in place before school starts. First, important training and professional development occur prior to the start of school. A teacher who is hired later will miss these. Additionally, teaching staff begin to bond and unite as a team prior to the start of the year and a teacher would miss this opportunity if hired late. Also, students learn procedures and expectations for behavior and learning at the beginning of the school year. A teacher who is hired late may have to reset expectations for students, which could cause a difficult start for both teacher and students.

Impact of Having Temporary Staff on the Instructional Program

At times it is necessary to have temporary staff to support the instructional program. If there is a teaching vacancy or if a teacher is absent for an extended period of time, a leader may have to obtain temporary personnel until a permanent solution is found. Often, however, temporary staff persons are not highly qualified and do not have the same training and experience that permanent staff members do. As a result, the quality of instruction may be reduced when temporary staff persons are in the classroom. Additionally, with temporary staff persons, there may be a need for increased monitoring and support from other permanent staff persons, such as clerks and administrators, to ensure the effective and efficient progress of the instructional program. This can produce further strain on staff and the instructional program. To ensure that the instructional program is excelling and that students are receiving high quality instruction, the school leader should minimize the need for temporary staff.

Impact of School Culture on Teacher Recruitment

School culture is determined by the leader and the staff of the campus. The school culture can create a welcoming environment for new teachers or it can repel them. When the school culture is positive, focused on students, and driven by excellence, teachers will want to be part of that culture. They will be motivated by the positive culture and will recruit others to join the team. Additionally, when the culture is positive, students thrive, which can make the teacher's job easier and more enjoyable. On the other hand, if the school culture is negative, teachers and staff will likely have negative attitudes as well. Teachers will seek a way out of that school environment rather than encouraging others to join the team. This negative culture can negatively affect student academic performance and behavior. If a potential teacher candidate observes a negative school culture, he or she may be unwilling to work at that campus.

Impact of Leadership Style on Teacher Recruitment

The leadership style of the school leader and other leaders on campus can positively or negatively impact teacher recruitment. A leadership style that is perceived as negative can deter teachers from wanting to work at that leader's campus. During the recruitment process, a candidate may observe how the school leader speaks to him or her, the way the leader treats staff and students, and other indicators of leadership style. For example, if a leader is perceived as being overly demanding, negative, or micromanaging, a teaching candidate will not want to work for him or her. In contrast, if a leader is fair, supportive, or warm, a teaching candidate will be attracted to the position. Effective leaders attract effective teachers. Teachers will seek to work on campuses where they will thrive and grow, and the school leader is an indication of whether the campus will meet a teacher's professional needs.

Seeking Community-Based and Other Additional Resources Needed for Accomplishing Goals

Seeking Additional Resources for Accomplishing Goals

A school leader may seek additional resources for accomplishing goals because there may not be sufficient school funding to accomplish everything that needs to be accomplished. When planning school budgets, leaders have to determine how to allocate funds. Often budgets have shortfalls, especially for initiatives that are lower on the priority list. As a result, a leader may have to seek funding and resources from outside of school to accomplish these goals. These additional resources may be in the form of grants, donations, volunteers, and many more. For example, if a school leader wanted to establish a garden on campus, rather than using school funds for the gardening supplies and staff to tend the garden, the leader may solicit donations of gardening tools and volunteers to work in the garden. These types of resources can be very beneficial to the instructional program and alleviate some of the constraints of the school budget.

The leader has the primary role in ensuring that sufficient resources are available to accomplish the set goals. First, the leader should properly allocate the funds and resources allotted by the school district to meet goals. If there is a shortfall in resources, the leader is responsible for advocating on behalf of the school to solicit additional resources. This may include petitioning for additional resources from the school district or seeking resources from community organizations and businesses. A leader may apply for grants to support the school program; seek donations of funds, resources, or equipment; or gather volunteers for staffing support. For example, if the school cannot afford to purchase new computers, a leader may ask a business organization to donate used computers to the school. The leader should take initiative in securing the resources necessary to accomplish the goals that he or she set for the school.

Potential Community-Based Resources

There are many community-based resources that are likely available to schools. For many communities, local churches offer a variety of resources that can support the school, such as volunteers, food and clothing for students and families in need, and much more. Also, many cities have local community programs to support the physical and mental health needs of the community and to provide nutritional support to families in need. There may be programs related to local transportation, arts, sciences, sports, clubs, and others that are available in the community. A school leader should be aware of all of the organizations in the surrounding community and communicate with these organizations to determine how they can partner to support students and their families. Often, these community-based resources can support students' non-instructional needs so that they can participate in the school program. These needs may include counseling, health-related needs, food and housing needs, and others.

Organizational and Systems Leadership

Types of Organizational Systems

Organizational Systems

A school organizational system refers to how a school is organized in relation to resources, personnel, time, and space to achieve student learning and success. Examples of school organizational models include departmental models, project-based learning models, academy models, integrative models, small community models, and the school-within-a school model, among others. The organizational system dictates the structure of the school and its systems, how personnel are allocated and what personnel are needed, what resources are needed, and how the physical space of the school is designed and utilized. Consequently, the organizational system in a school dictates how instruction is delivered and how student learning is achieved.

Types of School Organizational Systems

The different types of school organizational systems affect how instruction is delivered on campus. In the departmental model, the different subject or content areas are separated and distinct. Each of the subject-area departments have leaders or chairs who report to administration. In an integrative model, disciplines are combined or grouped together such as in the pairing of math and science classes or English and history classes. Project-based learning models facilitate interdisciplinary learning through student completion of large, extended projects. In academy models, a school may group students and classes based on college or career pathways. Small community models and school-within-a-school models are similar in that students are grouped into cohorts and remain within a small community for their instruction. Each community operates like a small school. In the school-within-a-school model, the small communities often have their own administrators. Other types of school organizational systems have developed as technology has become more accessible in schools, such as virtual schools and flipped classrooms.

Determining the Best Organizational System for a School

To determine the best organizational system for a school, a leader should first examine the school vision and goals. The organizational system should support the school vision and facilitate achievement of the school goals. For example, if the school is focused on reading performance and instruction, the leader may select a block scheduling structure to provide students with more instructional time in reading. A leader may also determine that, in order to provide socio-emotional support to students, dividing a large school into teams or houses would best facilitate relationship building and cultivate a small-school feel. A leader can also analyze the school's culture and identify the appropriate organizational system to support the ideal culture. For example, if the school vision is to create independent, life-long learners, the school organization system may involve giving students autonomy in their learning when possible. For example, the school could offer self-paced instructional programming, student course selection, and other exploratory opportunities for students.

Areas of Organizational Systems Not Directly Related to Classroom Instruction

Many organizational systems are part of the campus system but are not directly related to instruction. For example, the cafeteria represents a large system within the school. The process of feeding breakfast, lunch, and even dinner to students can be a complex organizational system. It involves providing the food, serving it, and maintaining the facilities in which it is served. This particular system may be regulated by state and federal regulations, which add additional complexities. Another organizational system is behavior management and discipline. There are processes in place to promote positive student behavior and deter negative behavior. This system may include the development and distribution of handbooks, training and communication regarding behavioral expectations, and imposing consequences for infractions. Other systems include student arrival and dismissal, extracurricular programming, counseling, and others. Even though these systems are not directly related to classroom instruction, they often support effective classroom instruction.

Systems Thinking

Systems thinking involves understanding how a system or an organization is constructed. It is an understanding of the many parts that make a system work, how those parts interact with one another, and how those parts relate to the larger context of the system. For example, the system of providing food to students in the cafeteria is one part of the larger campus system. A leader who understands systems thinking understands that how the cafeteria functions can directly or indirectly affect the way another system functions, such as the classroom. If the cafeteria is unable to serve breakfast efficiently in the morning, students may be delayed in getting to class, which in turn impacts instruction. Therefore, systems thinking helps in understanding how the organization or system as a whole can best function by improving the function of the smaller systems that make up the whole.

Short-Term and Long-Term Plans for Improving Organizational System

Considerations for Short-Term Improvement of the School's Organizational System

A leader should evaluate the school's organizational system for continuous, short-term improvements. Factors to consider include functionality, training, and resources. The organizational system should function smoothly and efficiently. This is indicated by student and staff transitions throughout the day as well as flow of information and resources. For example, if the school's organizational system is made up of small learning communities, it would be effective to place resources such as supplies and copiers near the learning communities. Also, the leader should ensure that staff has the appropriate training to support the organizational system. For example, if the organizational system is based on a project-based learning environment, staff will need appropriate, ongoing training to support this type of system. Finally, the leader should ensure that the school has the appropriate resources, both physical and human, to support the organizational system. This may include reassigning certain resources from one area of the school to another.

Considerations for Long-Term Improvement of a School's Organizational System

For long-term improvement of a school's organizational system, the leader should consider alignment to vision and goals, availability and allocation of resources, and spatial designs. First, the organizational system should support the school's vision. For example, a virtual school environment may not be appropriately aligned to a school vision that prioritizes building social and collaborative skills in students, due to its focus on individual, computerized work. Consequently, the leader needs to determine if the school's organizational system needs to be changed to reflect the changing needs of the students and community that the school serves. Next, the leader needs to determine the availability of both physical and human resources and how those are allocated to support the school's organizational system. This may require hiring additional staff, replacing or redesigning staff positions, or acquiring new resources such as technology devices. Finally, the leader needs to consider whether the layout and organization of the physical space in the school is conducive to the school's organizational system. To implement a school-within-a-school model, for example, the leader may need to redesign or relocate certain classrooms and offices.

Physical Plant Safety and Compliance with Regulations

Effects of Physical Plant Safety on the Instructional Program

Failure to ensure the physical safety of the school plant and comply with building regulations can negatively affect the instructional program. If students and staff are in danger of being injured or hurt due to aspects of the plant that are in disrepair or do not meet codes and standards, this can interrupt the school day and cause the school and school district to be liable. For example, if the school has an elevator in use that is not up to code, there is danger of a student or staff person becoming trapped in the elevator due to malfunction. This is dangerous to the person in the elevator and would necessitate emergency personnel, causing a disruption to the instructional program. Additionally, malfunctioning equipment such as leaks, loud machinery or A/C equipment, or pest infestations are distracting to the instructional environment and may cause damage to instructional resources such as books and technology equipment. Compliance with regulations, such as ADA codes, is important to ensure access of all students and staff, especially those with disabilities, to all areas of the campus.

Monitoring the Physical Plant for Safety and Compliance

A leader can monitor the physical plant for safety and compliance in several ways. First, a leader should have a plant operator who is responsible for ensuring the plant's safety and compliance. The leader should meet with the plant operator regularly to address any concerns that may arise. Second, the leader should conduct regular walks of the plant to inspect it for safety and compliance. During these walks, the leader should take note of plant aspects that may need repair or maintenance. Also, the leader may receive formal or informal feedback regarding needed repairs and maintenance from instructional staff. Finally, city or county officials will conduct regular inspections and provide reports. These reports will detail aspects of the campus that are in compliance, out of compliance, or in danger of being out of compliance with regulations. The school leader can use these reports to ensure the plant's safety and compliance.

Bond Referendum

A bond referendum is a proposal to borrow funds long-term to fund major capital improvements. Since these capital improvements are costly, the bond allows the expenses to be spread over time so that the costs are covered by current and future taxpayers. The bond must be approved by voters because of the obligation that taxpayers will have in paying for the expenses incurred by the capital improvements. Funds secured through a bond referendum can be used for construction of new schools or district facilities, renovation of existing schools or district facilities, and other updates related to the physical aspects of the plant. Bond funds can be used to help schools update their buildings to new city or county building codes, ADA requirements, and technology requirements. Construction due to capital improvements may cause the displacement of students and staff from certain areas of the school plant where construction occurs or, in more substantial projects, relocation to another setting until construction is completed.

Communication and Data Systems

Planning for Crises

Even though crises are unpredictable, a leader can plan in advance to ensure that the school is as prepared as possible. First, the leader should have emergency plans in place for events such as natural disasters, fire, medical emergencies, intruders on campus, etc. These plans should be written and key emergency staff should be trained on how to implement the plans in time of crisis. Additionally, the leader can implement drills to practice the crisis plans. The leader can evaluate staff and student performance during these drills and provide feedback to participants or revise the emergency plans based on the performance. The leader should also be familiar with district policies regarding emergency plans, drills, and reporting. A leader should make contact with local emergency services in the community to establish a relationship and ascertain important information and contacts to help in the event of an emergency or crisis.

Effective Data Systems

Effective data systems are important for managing the organizational systems on campus. Data systems relating to student and staff population data are essential to the effective planning and management of the organizational system. For example, staffing is often determined by the number of students enrolled in the school and the allocation of those enrollment numbers to various aspects of the instructional program, such as grade levels, special populations, magnet programming, and more. Leaders must have accurate data for student enrollment in order to allocate staff to the various programs on campus. This type of data also impacts class sizes and student to teacher ratios. Additionally, areas of the campus have capacity maximums as dictated by fire code and these limitations must be taken into consideration when planning lunch schedules, school assemblies, and other uses of school facilities. Effective data systems are also necessary to make decisions related to funding and resource acquisition and allocation, in addition to instructional decision-making.

Acquisition and Maintenance of Equipment and Technology

Determining What Equipment to Acquire and When

A leader must decide if new equipment is necessary for the effective operation of the physical plant as well as the implementation of the instructional program. A leader should be aware of the life expectancy of the various equipment that is already on campus so that he or she can determine when new equipment may be needed. This helps in the planning of maintenance, repair, and replacement cycles. Also, the leader must determine if equipment is mandatory or optional. Equipment that must be present on campus for its operation is prioritized over equipment that can be acquired or repaired at a later date. For example, a leader may need to postpone the acquisition of new science lab equipment in order to repair air conditioning units. School finances must also be considered when contemplating the acquisition of new equipment. A leader may need to postpone the purchase of major equipment until a new fiscal year due to budget constraints. The school leader should also consider the impact of the new equipment. If the purchase of new equipment will impact the majority of the students or staff, it can be placed higher on the priority list than equipment that may impact a small group of students, such as a student organization or specialized instructional program.

Role of Technology on Campus

Technology on campus impacts campus safety, communication, and instruction. Technology hardware and software are vital to the school. Technology can be used to assist with campus safety. For example, cameras are placed on campus to monitor activity. These cameras and the associated software necessary for monitoring and recording the camera feeds are important to school safety. Other technology used for safety includes intercom systems for screening of visitors, software to conduct background checks of visitors and volunteers, and automated door locking systems. Technology also aids in effective communication on campus. Emails, intercoms and radios, PA systems, marquees, and other forms of technology are used to communicate to staff and students. Also, technology is very useful for instruction. Computers, projectors, printers, and many other technology devices enhance the quality of instruction that is provided to students. Both staff and students may use these technology devices as part of the instructional routine.

Physical and Emotionally Safe Environments and Policy for Students and Staff

Physically Safe Environment

A physically safe environment is free from seen and unseen dangers that would pose a threat to the physical safety of anyone exposed to the environment. A physically safe environment is in good repair, accessible to all, and accommodating to its designated purpose. For example, a physically safe classroom would be free from damaged walls, ceilings, or floors; broken or damaged furniture; leaky pipes or plumbing; and electrical hazards. Additionally, a physically safe environment includes well-controlled people so that no one is physically harmed by the presence of others. This includes adhering to capacity limitations and monitoring the conduct of those present in the environment. For example, a school cafeteria should not exceed the posted maximum capacity of persons, even for special events, and persons should be able to move safely and freely in the cafeteria in accordance with its purpose.

Emotionally Safe Environment

An emotionally safe environment is an environment in which all persons are able to learn. This type of environment is free from all obstacles, emotions, and conflicts due to preventative strategies and quick resolutions. When an environment is not emotionally safe, children can feel fear, anxiety, and a host of other emotions. In an emotionally safe environment, both adults and children feel comfortable participating in the learning environment and interacting with one another. There is an absence of peer-to-peer and peer-to-adult conflict as well as bullying. Procedures and systems, such as counseling, mentoring, and other interventions, are in place to ensure the emotional safety of students on campus. There is an emphasis on communicating one's needs to foster active participation and engagement in the learning process. Additionally, the physical arrangement of the environment is designed to contribute to emotional safety, such as including windows and natural lighting, inspirational and positive posters and bulletin boards, and aesthetically pleasing furniture and decoration.

Ensuring the School Physical Plant, Equipment, and Support Systems Operate Safely, Efficiently, and Effectively

A leader must ensure that the school's physical plant, equipment, and support systems operate safely, efficiently, and effectively. The first step is to identify the appropriate staff to manage the physical plant. This person has the primary responsibility to ensure the safe functioning of everything on campus, so the leader must have the right person in place and must monitor his or her performance. Also, the leader must provide the plant manager with competent staff to support plant maintenance. In partnership with the manager, the leader can develop systems of monitoring and inspection to ensure that all aspects of the plant are running efficiently and safely. The school leader should also solicit feedback from other staff members who use certain aspects of the school plant. For example, if the school has a swimming pool, the leader should get feedback from the swimming coach or athletic director regarding the pool facilities. This feedback can help to identify areas of improvement, repair, or replacement needs.

Role That Local, State, and Federal Laws and Policies Play in Maintaining a Safe Environment

Local, state, and federal laws and policies help school leaders maintain a safe environment for students and staff. These regulations and policies, when adhered to, create a minimum level of safety. For example, federal laws regarding aspects of school safety such as asbestos management, ADA compliance, Internet safety, and others are interpreted into school policies. School districts may have additional safety requirements, such as the presence of police officers on campus, campus visitor policies, volunteer policies, and others. Local laws and policies may include fire codes and occupation limits, as well as other mandates for building safety that are not particular to schools but are implemented in all public places in the area. Each of these regulations and policies is meant to enhance the safety of the school, so the school leader should prioritize adherence to these regulations and policies. Failure to comply with local, state, and federal laws and policies can result in sanctions, fines, or other repercussions.

Maintaining a Physically Safe Environment for Students

A leader should take proactive steps to maintain a physically safe environment for students. First, the school leader should conduct regular inspection and maintenance of all parts of the building to ensure that no aspects of the physical building pose hazards to students. Next, the school leader should monitor flows of traffic within the school building to maintain safety. For example, a leader may notice that a school banner obstructs visibility in a hallway, causing students to bump into one another during transitions between classes. To promote safety, the leader should relocate the banner to a different area of the school. The leader should also ensure that common assembly areas such as hallways, courtyards, auditoriums, and others are monitored by school staff to prevent or identify conflict between students that could lead to physical harm.

Maintaining an Emotionally Safe Environment for Staff

Like the students, staff members need an emotionally safe environment. A leader can establish and maintain an emotionally safe environment through leadership style, communication, awareness, and support. When a leader has a caring and empathetic demeanor, employees will feel emotionally safe. In contrast, high-strung, micromanaging leaders can create fear and anxiety in staff. Also, leaders need to maintain open lines of communication with staff members. This allows them to communicate their needs so the leader can address them when possible. A leader should be able to recognize or be aware of aspects of the environment that endanger emotional safety for staff and should be able to address those concerns. For example, a lax discipline policy can create a challenging environment for teachers and staff. A leader can take steps to remedy this and create a safer environment. Finally, a leader should provide avenues of emotional support for staff. This may include staff counseling, referrals, or other accommodations and support that can help staff members feel emotionally safe.

Normative Behavior Expectations for Staff and Students

Role of Student Behavior in Maintaining a Safe Environment

Student behavior must be regulated and controlled for a safe school environment. Students who are unsupervised or do not adhere to established rules and procedures pose a threat to the safety of the school and to themselves. As a result, student behavior management is necessary to maintain a safe environment. School staff and ultimately the school leader are responsible for the safety of students the entire time they are at school. Unsupervised students may lead to an unsafe environment since they are less prone to follow rules when supervision is present. All students should be accounted for at all times and actively monitored. Additionally, students who misbehave can cause disruption, conflict, destruction of property, and a host of other actions that threaten the safety of the school environment. As a result, negative student behavior must be addressed quickly and effectively to maintain a safe environment.

Behavior Management and Discipline Strategies to Use to Manage Student Behavior

A leader may use a variety of behavior management and discipline strategies, as well as instructing staff to use them, to properly manage student behavior. These different techniques and strategies almost all have certain characteristics in common. Effective behavior management requires active supervision. It is not enough for adults to be present wherever students are. They must survey students, anticipate student behaviors, and be prepared to intervene when necessary. Also, most strategies require that adults set clear expectations for student behavior. This can be done through establishing rules, behavior contracts, or other ways to articulate expectations. Finally, there must be clear consequences, applied fairly and equitably, for behavioral infractions. Many behavior management strategies encourage building relationships and rapport with students, incorporating positive consequences for appropriate student behavior, and addressing student behaviors without overly emotional responses such as yelling, sarcasm, or unprofessional language.

Student Behavior Management and Student Success

Student behavior management and student success are related because poor student behavior detracts from the learning environment. If a student is behaving in a disruptive or disengaged way in the classroom, he or she cannot learn effectively. If the poorly-behaved student misses the instructional content, he or she will be less likely to succeed academically in that class. Poor student behavior can also negatively impact the academic success of other students in the room. For example, speaking out of turn, interrupting, and bothering others detracts from the learning environment. Finally, some behavioral consequences require the misbehaving student to be removed from the classroom. In these instances, the student often loses out on instructional opportunities, which can negatively impact academic success. Consequently, when student behavior is appropriately managed, the learning environment is preserved and all students have an opportunity to learn in a safe environment.

Importance of Fairness and Equity in Applying Student Behavior Management Principles

Student behavior management strategies and discipline must be applied in a fair and equitable manner to be effective and maintain a positive school environment. Fairness involves communicating expectations prior to applying discipline. If expectations are unknown or unclear, students can be frustrated and deem it unfair to be held responsible. Fairness also means that the adults adhere to the expectations and consequences that have been communicated to students and parents. For example, a behavior strategy may be to give a student a warning before applying consequences. A teacher may give students multiple warnings on one day and never give consequences for a particular behavior, but on another day, the teacher may immediately give a consequence for the same behavior without a warning. This type of inconsistent behavior from the teacher would be deemed unfair. Also, staff must practice equity in discipline. Adherence to written policies and procedures can ensure that all students are disciplined in an equitable manner, regardless of race, gender, or academic and behavioral history.

Emergency Situations and Support

Role of Procedures in Emergency Situations

Procedures are necessary in emergency situations to ensure the safety of everyone affected. In emergency situations, emotions can cloud thinking and judgment. Additionally, persons who are not familiar with a particular emergency situation may not know what to do in these instances. Having a procedure in place ensures that the right actions are taken in the event of an emergency, regardless of the emotional state or expertise of those involved. For example, if a person has a health emergency on campus, procedures should be in place for addressing the situation, including calling an ambulance, providing emergency aid, and maintaining the safety and order of the staff and students not immediately involved in the situation. These procedures should be taught to all staff on campus and be available in written form so it is accessible in the event of emergency. Having written procedures in place and abiding by them in the event of an emergency can also serve as legal protection for the school leader and staff.

Key Emergency Support Personnel Inside and Outside of the School

The school leader should identify key emergency support personnel on campus to prepare them for emergencies. These key staff members should know their roles in each emergency instance and be trained on how to fulfill those roles in the event of an emergency. These staff members may include the school nurse, counselor, police officer or security personnel, administrators or other school leaders, clerks, and others, depending on the nature of the emergency. For example, a different team of personnel may be needed to respond to a health emergency than a natural disaster emergency. Emergency support personnel outside of the school may include key district staff members and personnel at various emergency response organizations, such as the fire department.

Documentation and Communication in Emergency Situations

Emergency preparedness means that the school leader and staff have identified potential types of emergencies and planned the procedures, staff, and resources needed to address each type. Emergencies may include health emergencies, fire, natural disaster, intruders on campus, and many others. For each of these potential emergencies, a written plan of procedures should be created, detailing how everyone on campus should behave in the event of such an emergency. Key personnel with specific roles and responsibilities should be identified in the written plan. Everyone should be trained prior to the emergency to follow the written procedures. For many emergencies, practice drills can be conducted, such as fire drills or school lockdowns. Also, resources should be acquired, stored in designated locations, and inspected periodically. These resources may include printed copies of emergency procedures, fire extinguishers, automatic defibrillators, first aid kits, and other resources.

Promotion of Counseling and Health Referral Systems

Key Staff That Can Promote the Welfare of Staff and Students

The key staff member responsible for promoting the welfare of staff and students is the school leader. The school leader creates a school culture in which students and staff feel safe, as well as structures and systems to provide support and intervention for students and staff in need. The school leader also sets the example for treatment of students and staff, such as displaying understanding, empathy, and compassion. The school leader should also identify other key staff who can promote the welfare of staff and students. Each member of the leadership team, such as assistant principals or deans, should take the lead in promoting the welfare of all and lead by example. The school leader should also enlist the support of counselors, nurses, and others who can be proactive in identifying and responding to the needs of students and staff. Additionally, teachers play a key role in identifying the needs of students and promoting their welfare within the classroom.

Promoting Counseling and Wellness

A leader should promote counseling and wellness to encourage staff and students to take advantage of these supports for their own welfare. A leader can do this by making counseling and wellness programs visible to all. This may mean having signs and displays around the school that promote these programs. Also, the leader can communicate the availability of these resources using common means of communication, such as emails, news bulletins, school public announcements, and announcements in staff meetings. The staff members who lead counseling and wellness programs can be included in other school projects and programs, such as in behavior intervention meetings or academic interventions, so that they are viewed as an integral part of the campus team. A school leader can also consider hosting mental health and wellness fairs for school members and the community to raise awareness about potential health concerns and to promote available services.

Indicators That Staff May Need Counseling and Health Referrals

A leader can watch for several indicators to determine that staff members may need a recommendation to counseling and health services. Teachers and staff who need help may be frequently absent without a reasonable excuse. These absences may be jokingly referred to as "mental health days" but are often indicators that a staff person is stressed or overwhelmed. Another indicator of a need for counseling and health services are overly emotional responses to everyday stimuli. These responses may include yelling, crying, or bursts of anger. The school leader can also look for changes in staff behavior. For example, if a staff member who is usually outgoing, energetic, and talkative becomes withdrawn and disengaged, this may indicate a need for additional support. Staff who are unable to do their jobs satisfactorily, especially if they have a history of satisfactory performance, may need support from counseling and health services. The school leader should keep communication open so that staff are comfortable communicating that they need help.

Indicators That Students May Need Counseling and Health Referrals

A leader can watch for several indicators to determine that students may need a recommendation to counseling and health services. A student may begin to act out and display negative behaviors in the classroom with other students or with adults on campus. This can be an indicator if the student does not usually display poor behavior at school. Additionally, a student who is usually engaged in classroom activities and with peers but becomes withdrawn and disengaged may also need help. These indicators can also lead to poor academic performance, indicated by falling grades. Students in need of support may also demonstrate emotional responses in school such as angry outbursts, crying, yelling, or even physical altercations with other students. In some instances, a parent may communicate with a staff member that the child is having difficulty at home as well. A school leader should ensure that systems are in place on campus to allow students to express their needs so that they can be referred for services. This may include having walk-in counseling hours or open-door policies with key staff members.

Making Reports to Child Protective Services

Child Protective Services is a service provided by state agencies to protect the welfare of children. This agency investigates allegations of child abuse or neglect and provides services to children should such allegations be proven valid. There will be instances in which the school leader or a school staff member has reason to believe that a child is being neglected or abused. Whenever there is suspicion of abuse or neglect, it is each staff person's responsibility, including the school leader's, to submit a formal report to Child Protective Services for investigation. For example, if a teacher reports to the school leader that one of her students has confided that his or her mother is hitting him or her with various objects and shows the teacher bruises, both the teacher and the leader should file a report. There can be legal ramifications for staff members who fail to report suspected child abuse or neglect.

Being Proactive in Promoting the Wellness of Staff and Students

Being proactive in promoting the wellness of staff and students means that the leader is actively looking for ways to maintain the wellness of all before problems arise. This is important because prevention is often more effective and less costly than trying to address a problem after it has already occurred. For example, taking steps to prevent teen suicide is a better course of action than addressing a grieving student body after a teen has committed suicide. Similarly, it is more effective to help an unwell teacher obtain needed help than to lose the teacher for the remainder of the school year due to a health crisis. The school leader should proactively promote wellness and identify potential wellness needs among students and staff so that mental health crises can be prevented or at least detected early in an effort to prevent tragedies that directly affect the student body and staff. Being proactive demonstrates to all that the leader is concerned about the wellness of staff and students and is willing to take the needed steps to address their health concerns.

Helping Staff and Students Deal with Grief on Campus

At times the student body and staff members will experience the loss of a peer or colleague. In these instances, the school leader will need to implement strategies to address the grief that students and staff experience. The first step that the leader must take is to acknowledge the loss. The leader should not operate with a "business-as-usual" attitude. Many schools have access to grief counselors who can be present on campus to assist students or staff who need assistance in dealing with their emotions. The school leader should also demonstrate understanding and compassion during this time and recognize that grief may cause students or staff to behave out of character, such as missing school, expressing outbursts of emotion like sadness or anger in school, or being disengaged from academic activities. It is important to listen to the needs of the students and staff during this time. The leader may provide opportunities for students and staff to express their feelings or to honor the one who has died.

Preventing Teen Suicide

The school leader can take steps to aid in the prevention of teen suicide or self-harm. Although many factors and influences outside of the school can lead a young person to commit suicide, the school and its staff can serve as a resource and support to students who experience suicidal thoughts. First, the leader should create a school culture in which students feel comfortable turning to teachers and staff for support. When this type of culture is present, a student is more likely to share thoughts of self-harm with a staff member, which can aid in prevention. The school should also have counseling staff and resources available for students who are experiencing emotional issues. Many schools discuss this topic with the student body and provide telephone hotline numbers for support 24 hours a day. Also, if an adult becomes aware that a student is contemplating suicide or self-harm, he or she has a duty to report it to the proper authorities.

Role Social Media Plays in Student Wellness and Mental Health

Social media has a large influence on students' wellness and mental health. Students who engage in social media often experience negative emotions as a result. Some students develop feelings of inadequacy or low self-esteem when they compare themselves to others online. This is the result of unrealistic beauty expectations and exaggerated portrayals of others' lives. Additionally, students may be exposed to cyberbullying via social media. This type of bullying can involve name calling, threats, shaming, spreading rumors, and other negative behaviors that can negatively impact a student's well-being. Cyberbullying can lead to bullying and other conflict on campus as well. Finally, engaging in social media can be addictive for some youth. They may spend excessive amounts of time on social media or engage in risky behaviors in an attempt to gain social media attention. For example, a student may post provocative pictures of him or herself in an effort to attract attention. This can have negative consequences for the student's mental health and overall wellness.

Leader's Own Physical and Mental Wellness

In addition to ensuring the wellness of students and staff, the school leader should take steps to ensure his or her own physical and mental wellness. A leader cannot fulfill job responsibilities properly if he or she is not well. Also, the school leader should set an example for staff and students by prioritizing personal health needs. This is primarily accomplished by being proactive instead of waiting until a health problem arises to address it. First, the leader should delegate responsibilities and accept assistance whenever possible to keep stress levels low. The leader should also get regular checkups to quickly identify potential health problems. Eating and sleeping properly are also key components of maintaining physical and emotional health. Finally, the school leader should take advantage of the resources and supports that are offered on campus and through the school district. These may include counseling, use of workout facilities, support groups, nurse hotlines, and many other resources designed to support the physical and mental health of staff.

Resources for Promoting Wellness

Utilizing Community Services for Staff and Student Welfare

It is important for a school leader to utilize community services for staff and student welfare because school funds and resources are often insufficient to provide abundant resources for staff and students. Even if a school has sufficient budgetary resources, there is no need to spend funds on resources that may be available as a free community service. Also, utilizing community services may expand the number and type of resources that are available, which means more support and help for members of the school community. Most school services only provide services directly to students, whereas community services often have programs, resources, and support for the entire family, which can be more impactful to students and their families in many instances. Finally, utilizing community services builds partnerships and relationships between the school and the community, which can have long-range benefits for both parties. For example, schools and community organizations can partner in community events, student recruitment, and applications for grant funding.

Identifying Community Resources for Promoting Wellness

A leader can identify community resources for promoting wellness in a variety of ways. Often, these organizations desire to partner with the school and will visit or call the school to inform campus leadership of their services and identify ways that they can serve the school community. Sometimes school district offices maintain directories of community organizations and programs that support students and their families within the school district. The school leader can also do a basic Internet search to identify nearby resources. Local resources include branches of city, county, or state organizations and are easily identified online. Finally, the school leader can make an effort to venture into the community and make connections with the leaders of area organizations to determine how the school and the organizations can collaborate.

Discipline Policy and Conflict Resolution

Discipline

Discipline is training students to abide by a specific code of behavior. When discipline is present, rules are typically stated and taught and expectations for behavior are defined in a variety of contexts and situations. In addition to the rules that are outlined as part of the discipline policy, there are consequences associated with failing to abide by the stated rules and expectations for behavior. Many associate discipline with administering consequences for failing to follow rules. However, the essence of discipline is the practice of training or teaching behavior. In schools, rules are often set by the school district and written in a student code of conduct for district-wide discipline. Schools may also have campus-wide expectations for behavior as part of their discipline, as well as sets of rules for individual classrooms. When discipline is effective, students are fully aware of behavior expectations and the consequences associated with not meeting those expectations.

Promoting Conflict Resolution

Conflict resolution is the practice of resolving conflicts or disagreements, such as verbal or physical altercations, between students to prevent further disruption. To promote conflict resolution, staff members must be vigilant in identifying potential conflicts among the student body. Early intervention is essential in resolving conflicts effectively. Staff members also want to build relationships with students and create an environment in which students feel comfortable reporting conflicts to adults. Both persons experiencing the conflict should feel that there is an adult on campus who is willing and able to help them to resolve the conflict. There should be structures or systems in place to practice conflict resolution, which can include identifying mediators, locating neutral spaces for conversations between the conflicted parties, including parents and guardians, and support services to meet students' mental health needs. Additionally, the campus culture should utilize and promote conflict resolution, rather than simply administering consequences. This can be done by promoting conversations between students and adults and among peers regarding various aspects of their school experiences.

Applying Discipline Policy in a Fair and Equitable Manner

The school discipline policy must be applied to students in a fair and equitable manner. Many studies have shown that male students, especially minority males, are disciplined more often and more severely than their peers. Unfair discipline can lead to increased misbehavior from students who receive the discipline at a higher rate than others, as well as by students who witness the inequitable discipline. The student who is disciplined more frequently may believe that he or she will receive consequences regardless of behavior, so he or she may choose to misbehave and earn the consequences. Students who witness this may believe they will not be punished for their behavior, so they can behave however they like. Rules should be enforced consistently. For example, if a school rule states that students should not chew gum, this rule should be enforced at all times and with all students, not just when it is convenient for the teacher or other staff member. Additionally, applying discipline in an unfair or unequitable manner can damage relationships with students and parents and can negatively influence the school culture.

Communicating the School's Discipline Policy to Students, Staff, and Parents

The school's discipline policy should be communicated to students, staff, and parents. Students must understand behavioral expectations if they are to meet them. It cannot be assumed that all students and their families hold the same expectations for behavior. As a result, the school's discipline policy must be clearly communicated. This can be done with a printed handbook for student behavior, as well as through verbal communication. When the discipline policy is not communicated clearly, this can lead to confusion and anger when consequences are administered. Emotional reactions from students and their parents or guardians can be expected when consequences are administered, especially for severe consequences. Ambiguity around rules and consequences makes it difficult to administer discipline and can lead to the nullification of warranted consequences due to ineffective communication of the discipline policy.

Bullying

Bullying occurs when one uses strength or other means of influence to intimidate another person. Bullying can be verbal, social, or physical and involves an imbalance of power. To prevent bullying, a school leader must employ several strategies. First, students and staff must be aware of what bullying is and is not. This will help to identify bullying quickly if it occurs. Also, the leader should create an environment in which bullying is not acceptable or tolerated. This will encourage those who are being bullied and those who observe bullying to report it so that it can be stopped. The school leader and the staff should also model healthy, respectful relationships with one another. The leader should not be a bully to staff, nor should staff bully students, as this would set an inappropriate model for students on campus. Additionally, acts of bullying should be addressed swiftly and effectively. This may include disciplinary consequences or other interventions such as peer mediation, counseling, or other strategies.

Mild and Normal Disciplinary Problems

Common Disciplinary Problems

Many disciplinary issues among students are common and can be prepared for with effective classroom management strategies. One category of common discipline problems is disengagement. Students who disengage are not usually disruptive of others in the instructional setting but are not receiving instruction. These students may put their heads down and sleep or participate in off-task activities such as drawing, reading, writing, or daydreaming. Another category of discipline problems is disruptive. These behaviors indicate that the misbehaving student is not participating in instruction, and is additionally preventing others from participating. These behaviors include excessive talking, standing or walking around at inappropriate times, calling out, touching or hitting others, making disruptive noises, and many others. These types of behavior are often addressed by the teacher when they occur and do not require serious disciplinary consequences unless the behaviors are repeated and the student does not respond to redirection.

Using Restorative Justice in Schools

Restorative justice is a practice in which students who have harmed their school community or an individual through their misbehavior are required to repair the harm. The first step is to facilitate a conversation regarding the offender's behavior. This is usually led by an adult in the school. The offender has the opportunity to provide his or her side of the story and give input on the consequences. Traditional consequences usually include detention, suspension, and expulsion, among others, whereas restorative justice provides an opportunity for a holistic approach to correcting the misbehavior, "righting a wrong" or "making it right" and preventing it from recurring in the future. There are no predefined consequences, as these might vary significantly, based on the individual incident. For example, if a student has a temper tantrum, flips a desk in a classroom, and overturns a supply table, a community of adults and peers may determine that the student must clean the classroom during lunch for a week in addition to offering a public apology to the teacher and classmates.

Classroom Management

Classroom management refers to the strategies that teachers use to maintain order in the classroom and establish an environment conducive to learning. Classroom management is effective in preventing and addressing minor disciplinary problems. A teacher who demonstrates effective classroom management considers student behavior and management in all aspects of the instructional process, including lesson planning, lesson delivery, room arrangement, procedures, and more. For example, a teacher may use diverse instructional practices to engage students and prevent disengagement or off-task behavior during a lesson. A teacher may also design a lesson so that students can get out of their seats and move to different areas of the classroom at various points. Classroom management also involves having clear expectations for student behavior, established procedures for all instructional activities, and strategies for effective redirection of students who misbehave. Teachers with effective classroom management also build rapport with students and utilize parental communication to preserve the learning environment.

Different Discipline Approaches

School discipline approaches range from lax to very stringent. A lax approach does not mean that school discipline does not exist; it means that discipline is often determined on an individual basis, reflective of the circumstances and individuals involved. This may include practices such as teen or peer courts and restorative justice models. Some discipline approaches combine individualized disciplinary strategies with set disciplinary policies. These approaches may offer flexibility in disciplinary options for relatively minor offenses and more defined options for more severe offenses. The most stringent discipline approaches have strict, pre-determined consequences for student misbehaviors. The most common example of this type of discipline approach is a zero-tolerance policy. In zero-tolerance policies, the consequences associated with particular behavioral infractions are administered without regard to the individual offender, context, or other variables within the situation. Many schools implement discipline approaches that fall within the midrange of this continuum, but a school leader should determine the best discipline approach for the campus based on student needs.

Role of Parental Communication in Addressing Discipline Problems

Parental communication is an asset when addressing student discipline problems. It is important that parents are aware of their children's behavior while at school. This awareness, fostered through consistent and effective communication between the school and the parent, can help build a positive relationship and rapport. Additionally, the parent can support the school in disciplinary efforts and vice versa to establish consistency in behavioral expectations of the student. Finally, communication provides parents with the opportunity to intervene in a child's misbehavior before those behaviors escalate to more severe behaviors or have a negative impact on the student's academic progress. Failure to communicate with a parent regarding a child's behavior can cause negative consequences for the school, such as complaints about how the discipline was handled by school administration or contesting of assigned consequences. Parents or guardians should always be part of the disciplinary process.

Severe Disciplinary Problems

Role of Special Education Status in Addressing Disciplinary Problems

When a student who is identified as receiving special education services displays behavioral issues, it is important to take certain steps to meet the child's needs. Some students with this identification already have behavioral plans in place. Teachers and school leaders must abide by these plans, which may include specific strategies for correcting a student's behavior or predetermined disciplinary consequences decided by the special education committee, which may or may not be aligned to the general student code of conduct. If a student who receives special education services commits a severe disciplinary infraction that could warrant consequences such as suspension or expulsion, a special meeting must be held by the special education committee to determine if the behavior was a manifestation of the student's identified disability. If it is concluded by the committee that the behavior is a manifestation of the student's identified disability, that student would likely not be subject to the traditional disciplinary consequences outlined by the student code of conduct. On the other hand, if the committee determines that the student's behavior is not associated with the disability, the student would likely be subject to the outlined disciplinary consequences.

Role of Disciplinary Alternative Education Programs

Suspension and expulsion are consequences for severe student behavioral infractions. Suspensions typically last one to three days, but for some offenses, students are removed from the traditional education setting for longer periods of time. The public school system provides a means of education for all students, even those who have been removed from their traditional school due to extended suspension or expulsion. Students in these situations may receive their education through an alternative education program. In these programs, students may be assigned to attend the program for a certain number of days, usually for no longer than a school year. School districts may establish alternative education programs within the district or work with a program operating in that region. Additionally, students who commit crimes punishable by law may attend a school operated by the local juvenile justice department. Like other alternative education programs, the assigned duration that a student must attend varies based on the offense, as deemed by the courts.

Role of Law Enforcement in School Discipline

Some student behavioral infractions are not only violations of school codes of conduct, but also of the law. Consequently, law enforcement has the right and responsibility to administer legal consequences in addition to local disciplinary consequences. For example, if students engage in a physical altercation on campus, they are subject to local disciplinary consequences which may include suspension, but they are also subject to the law, which may warrant a citation. Many school districts and school leaders have opted to maintain a police presence on campus at all times. A school district may have its own police department dedicated to its schools. This police presence is established for the safety of everyone on campus, but if students break the law, the police exercise their authority by addressing the infraction. The involvement of law enforcement is discretionary, at times, depending on the offense. Law enforcement is not a replacement for school discipline, but a supplement.

Connecting the School Community with Federal, State, and Local Policy, Regulations, and Other Requirements

Participating in Professional Education Organizations and Associations

It is important for school leaders to participate in professional education organizations and associations. Many organizations have been created to support educators in various stages of their career. There are organizations primarily created for teachers in the classroom, even organizations specific to particular content areas. There are also organizations created specifically for school administrators. Additionally, school leaders may consider joining organizations related to the field in which they obtained their degree. These organizations provide training, information, and networking opportunities. Some offer legal help and protection as well. Most organizations charge a fee for membership and members have access to a website, newsletters, training opportunities, job postings and leads, networking events and much more. The information provided through these organizations can also help school leaders stay current on trends in education, changing laws and policies, and politics that affect the field of education. Additionally, networking within these professional organizations can provide opportunities for growth, advancement, and partnerships.

Use of Professional Influence to Impact the School

The school leader often has influence in the community due to the position of leadership. This influence comes from the connection to others who are in a position to support the school's vision and goals. Additionally, the size and diversity of a school leader's network and contacts can increase the power of that influence. The school leader's professional influence can be used to bring positive attention and resources to the school. For example, a school leader may know professional athletes, musicians, or actors within the community and can invite them to speak to or mentor the students on campus. Having such persons on campus can inspire the youth and encourage them to succeed academically. The school leader can also use his or her influence to secure opportunities for students from businesses and organizations in the community, such as field trips, internships, or other educational opportunities. Finally, the school leader's professional influence can be used to promote social justice within the school and the community. For example, the school leader may advocate for a public library within the community.

Sphere of Influence

A sphere of influence refers to a leader's power to affect others, even without formal authority. School leaders have authority over staff and students. Staff can be reprimanded or terminated and students can be disciplined. Staff and students conform their behavior to the expectations of the leader because of the leader's authority over them. In contrast, the leader does not have authority over parents, community members, district personnel, and other stakeholders. However, the leader has the ability to influence these persons through speech and other communication, as well as behavior. For example, a school leader cannot mandate that a neighborhood organization offer childcare services on campus after school because the school leader has no authority over that neighborhood organization. Instead, the school leader could use his or her influence to encourage or persuade the neighborhood organization to provide childcare services in partnership with the school. A school leader must recognize that when operating within the sphere of influence, skills such as understanding, compromise, persuasion, and clear communication are necessary to reach desired outcomes. This skillset differs from the skills used with those under the school leader's authority.

Educating Community Stakeholders About Local Education Processes

The purpose of educating community stakeholders about local education processes is to help them understand the reason for local policies and procedures and to help them engage in the local education processes. Community stakeholders who are uninformed or misinformed on local education processes may mistakenly assign responsibility or culpability to the school and school leader. Stakeholders should be aware of the decision-makers within the school district, the processes for decision-making, and how they can participate in those processes. This can help stakeholders to be effective in enacting change for decisions and processes that they do not agree with. For example, the school's dance program may be eliminated. Stakeholders may mistakenly believe that this was the school leader's decision when, in reality, the school district eliminated funding for these types of programs district-wide. Stakeholders should be educated regarding the budgeting process and how they can participate in the decision-making for district and school budgets.

Educating Community Stakeholders About State and Federal Education Processes

The purpose of educating community stakeholders about state and federal education processes is to help them understand the reason for the laws and policies that govern the education system and to help them engage in the state and federal processes. Many school policies and procedures are developed in response to state and federal laws. When community stakeholders are aware of the laws that impact their children, they are more likely to engage in the processes to affect change. For example, a community may believe that their students should not be subject to standardized testing. Those community members would need to be informed of the accountability laws that require assessment of students. Then the community members would be able to participate in the processes that could affect those laws in the future, such as voting.

Facilitating Discussions That May Lead to Identifying Areas in Need of Improvement

Value of Facilitating Discussions with Students

Students can help the school leader identify areas of the school in need of improvement from the student perspective. This perspective is invaluable when evaluating school programming and school culture. For example, the school leader may have instituted an art program for students based on the perception that students wanted more arts on campus. Students can inform the school leader how well that art program meets their needs. They may explain that the student body was interested in digital arts rather than classical arts, therefore making the school leader's art program ineffective. Students have to abide by the rules and policies that school leaders design and can often provide feedback on how effective those rules and policies are. Students can inform the school leader of aspects of the school that do not enhance school safety, are deemed unfair or inequitable, or are simply ineffective. Students are also helpful in providing solutions for areas of improvement on campus.

Value of Facilitating Discussions with Teachers

Teachers can help the school leader identify areas of the school in need of improvement from their perspective. Teachers are responsible for implementing the school program the leader designs. As a result, they are often aware of needed areas of improvement that the school leader cannot see. When a school leader facilitates discussions on school improvement with teachers, they are in a position to gather information that they may not have discovered otherwise. For example, the teachers may point out a misalignment in the curriculum's scope and sequence and the assessment calendar, which causes the performance data to be skewed. This information can help the leader analyze data that has already been collected and devise a plan for revising the assessment calendar. Additionally, including teachers in this discussion increases buy-in. This process allows them to voice their concerns and to identify areas of the school program that need improvement for them to do their job more easily and effectively.

Value of Facilitating Discussions with Community Stakeholders

Community stakeholders can provide the school leader with the community perspective of school areas in need of improvement. The school is an integral part of the community and plays a significant role in meeting the needs of community families. Community stakeholders can inform the school leader of areas in which the school is not meeting those needs. For example, community members may inform the school leader that school dismissal procedures are inadequate and that the school is creating disruptive traffic congestion in the community at dismissal time. The school leader can work with community members to develop a plan that is appropriate for the school and respectful of the surrounding community. Engaging community stakeholders in discussions relating to the efficacy of the school program also creates buy-in of the school vision and goals, as well as building relationships between the school and the community.

Value of Facilitating Discussions with District Personnel

Feedback from district personnel regarding areas of campus improvement is valuable. District personnel offer a unique perspective because they are able to view the school as it relates to the entire district's curricular program, mission, and goals. As a result, their perspective can help the school leader remain in alignment with district expectations. District personnel can also provide feedback based on how the school compares to other schools in the district. School leaders do not often have the opportunity to visit all the other schools within the district to gather ideas and best practices, but other district personnel can provide this perspective. Additionally, district personnel are often the persons responsible for evaluating the school leader's performance. Addressing weak areas identified by district personnel can ensure that the leader is meeting the district's performance expectations.

Root Cause Analysis

Conducting a root cause analysis involves identifying the root cause or underlying source of a problem. A root cause analysis begins with identifying the problem, then systematically identifying the source of that problem with the understanding that a sequence of events or chain of causes and effects may have led to the problem's manifestation. Conducting a root cause analysis is valuable because the main source of the problem can be addressed rather than just the symptoms. For example, the school leader may notice that math scores are below expectation. A further analysis of the data may indicate that the majority of the low performing students have their math class in the morning. A further analysis may indicate that a significant number of students arrive late to school every day and are missing the math instruction needed to perform well on the assessments. The school leader may conclude that addressing the tardiness may help to improve math scores. Root cause analysis helps the school leader to address the right problem in order to improve outcomes.

SWOT Analysis

A SWOT analysis is a method of identifying the strengths and weaknesses of an organization in order to develop an improvement plan. SWOT stands for Strengths, Weaknesses, Opportunities, and Threats. The strengths of an organization are what provide the school with a competitive advantage over other schools. A school may be technology-rich, which is a strength. Weaknesses describe areas of disadvantage relative to other schools. A school may have a poor attendance rate in comparison to other schools. Opportunities are areas the school may be able to use by leveraging strengths to address weaknesses. The school may identify that the technology can be used to provide students with instruction at home when absent or to provide accelerated instruction when they return to school. Threats are aspects of the environment that the school has little or no control over but may negatively affect the school. The school may identify that the closure of a chemical plant has resulted in the layoff of many students' parents. Conducting a SWOT analysis is helpful in identifying areas of potential improvement, even for schools that are already high-performing.

Areas of School Programming That Should Be Evaluated for Weaknesses

All areas of school programming should be evaluated for weaknesses. Academic performance is most often evaluated because this is the basis for school accountability measures. A school leader should examine the alignment of curriculum to assessments, the quality of the instruction that is delivered, and the rigor at which it is delivered. However, other aspects should also be evaluated. These include school safety, school culture, parental and family engagement, and much more. For example, a school leader should determine if school safety procedures are up-to-date and should also assess the performance of students and staff during safety drills. School culture can be evaluated based on student and staff perceptions as well as by the experiences and feedback of visitors on campus. Also, the school leader can identify whether the school is achieving family engagement on campus, if it is in the desired areas, and if it is producing the desired outcomes. There are always aspects of the school program that can be improved, so the school leader should have a mindset of continuous improvement.

Using Data to Identify Areas of Weakness

Data is essential in the identification of weaknesses in the school program. Differences and changes in the data, identifying potential areas of improvement, may be observed. The school leader may identify disparities in the data between the school and others in the district. For example, the school leader may note that on a district benchmark assessment, his or her school had the lowest overall performance. Based on that data, the leader could develop a plan for improvement. Data may also reveal a disparity in performance on campus from one school year to the next, or between various groups of students. Other data that can be used to identify areas of needed improvement include student attendance data, discipline data, compliance in data reporting, staff performance or evaluation data, and more. All data collected on campus has the potential to indicate needed improvements in the school program. The school leader should analyze the data in comparison to other data as well as changes, trends, and gaps in the data.

Encouraging Stakeholders to Lobby and Use Political Activism to Bring About Change

Encouraging Stakeholders to Lobby and Use Political Activism to Bring About Change

The school leader has the influence to encourage stakeholders to lobby and use political activism to bring about change, especially in regard to social justice. The primary way that the leader can encourage engagement is by educating the community on present issues. The leader often has several opportunities to speak to community families en masse. These opportunities can be used to educate families about education trends and politics that will ultimately affect their community, school, and families. By promoting awareness, the leader can empower parents and community members to become active. The second way the school leader can encourage engagement is by showing community stakeholders how they can become involved. The school leader can invite community stakeholders to be active in bringing about change by writing letters, sending emails, making phone calls, or engaging with political leaders.

Precautions to Take When Engaging in Political Activities

In the school leader's efforts to advocate for students and for social justice, the school leader must engage carefully. Most school districts have guidelines for how a school leader can represent him or herself in the community while representing the school district. These guidelines usually apply in regard to supporting specific political parties or candidates, persuading others how to vote in elections, and various other activities. A school leader must identify what actions they are allowed or not allowed to take while in the position of leader. Outside of school hours, the leader may have additional freedom to engage in such activities, but must still be aware of how his or her influence and authority are used in such activities. The school leader should consult with the school district or the leadership of their professional organizations regarding the implications of political engagement prior to doing so.

Current Trends in Education

Technology

One-to-One Technology Model

The one-to-one technology model is the practice of providing a technology device to each student on campus. As technology use has increased in schools, access to technology has been a focal point to aid in student performance and growth. In many instances, school leaders calculate the ratio of computers or technology devices to students. For example, the school may purchase enough computers to ensure that there is one computer for every 10 students. When there are not enough technology devices on campus for every student, computer and Internet access may be limited due to the need to share technology devices on campus. This may be done by equipping classrooms with a limited number of computers, making laptop carts available, or creating computer labs, all of which must be shared by teachers and students. With the one-to-one technology model, the ratio of technology to students is one device for each student. This allows maximum access to technology on campus. These technology devices are usually personal laptop computers or tablets. In some instances, the students are entrusted with the technology and are permitted to take the devices home for technology access outside of school hours.

Bring-Your-Own-Device Technology Model

The bring-your-own-device technology model describes the practice of allowing students to bring their own technology devices to school for use in classroom instruction. Many families provide their children with computers, tablets, and phones that can access the Internet. When this model is implemented, students can bring these devices to school and use them to participate in computer-based or web-based activities. The bring-your-own-device model is beneficial because it saves schools from purchasing the number of technology devices necessary for every student to have access. The downside of this model is that the school is not responsible for the care or repair of students' devices, not all students have a device, and there is often difficulty in designing lessons compatible with various types of technology. For example, there are different specifications for playing videos on tablets, laptops, and phones, which can be challenging to a teacher attempting to incorporate videos into the lesson. Also, this model has limited efficacy in impoverished communities, in which the majority of students do not have access to these devices.

Virtual School Model

The virtual school model is the practice of providing online courses to students, using a web-based platform or other computer-based program rather than physically attending a class. A student has access to instructional content online and participates in activities and tests to assess learning. In some virtual school models, students have virtual access to a teacher. In other models, the computer program is automated and student progress may be self-paced. Virtual school has been used in all grade levels as a supplement to traditional instruction or as a replacement. Virtual school can also be utilized for students who are home schooled. When used as a supplement to traditional classes, students may use virtual school to make up failed courses, participate in tutorials or interventions, or to access courses that are not offered on campus. The virtual school model requires that students have access to a technology device and Internet service. Many businesses also develop platforms and coursework for virtual schools. Most commonly, courses focus on the core content areas of reading, math, social studies, and science, but many learning platforms offer electives and tutorial programs.

Blended Learning

Blended learning is the process of incorporating technology use into traditional classroom instruction. In the blended learning model, teachers identify places in the lesson that can be supplemented with technology or in which technology can be used to drive the lesson. In this model, the teacher may use the technology in the lesson, but the focus is on students utilizing technology in the classroom. For example, a teacher may deliver content on a topic and then assess students' understanding with an online assessment tool. In the blended learning model, technology can be used to deliver content, such as accessing information through reading and videos or by creating slideshows or other presentations. Technology can be used to assess student learning as well. Blended learning models are often paired with project-based learning models. This allows students the freedom and opportunity to use the technology with limited guidance by the teacher to meet lesson objectives. In the blended learning model, technology use is flexible, so it may vary by content area or lesson as teachers still implement traditional instructional strategies.

School Discipline

Role of Meditation in Schools

Meditation is the act of engaging in quiet and silent thought or reflection. This practice has been used in schools as a strategy for redirecting poor student behavior. When a student breaks a school rule or disrupts class, rather than discipline with in-school suspension, out-of-school suspension, or other traditional consequences, the student is instructed to meditate. When students are given the opportunity to meditate, they are placed in a quiet environment where they can focus on calming down, breathing, and thinking about appropriate behaviors to display. Schools that have implemented meditation as a discipline strategy have seen a decrease in suspension rates and fewer discipline referrals from teachers. The practice of meditation is thought to alleviate emotional issues such as anxiety, anger, depression, and frustration, which could be sources of student misbehavior.

Challenges of Promoting School Safety

It is a school leader's primary responsibility to keep students safe while at school. This responsibility can be challenging for a variety of reasons. Recent acts of school violence have caused educators and government officials to revisit laws, policies, and procedures relating to school safety. In some schools, metal detectors are used to promote school safety, but some deem that practice to be controversial. As schools are built or remodeled, school designs include limited entrances and exits to the school building and compartmentalized front office areas that can prevent unauthorized persons from gaining entrance into the school. Other strategies include staffing uniformed police officers on campus during school hours, implementing standardized dress, and limiting backpacks and other large bags on campuses. Additionally, many schools practice drills for emergencies, such as having an intruder on campus. Promoting school safety is challenging because even the best preventative measures cannot guarantee that nothing will threaten the safety of students and staff.

Curricular Programming

Accelerated Learning

Accelerated learning is the practice of delivering content to students at an accelerated pace. For example, a traditional high school course that is delivered during an 18-week semester may be condensed into six or nine weeks. The purpose of accelerated learning is to provide students with additional learning opportunities. For example, if a student is already proficient in math, it can be reasoned that he or she should not have to sit through an 18-week course. Accelerated learning is also useful for students who have previously taken a course but were unsuccessful. These accelerated classes may be offered during summer breaks or built into the school's instructional program. Accelerated programs are often facilitated with technology-based programs, which can personalize and deliver content based on a student's needs. For example, a student enrolled in an accelerated course may take a pre-assessment online and then be assigned coursework based on assessment performance. A student would not have to complete coursework in areas of the course in which mastery is demonstrated.

School-Within-a-School Model

A school-within-a-school model describes the creation of a specialized school program to be operated on the same campus as the traditional school program. The students participating in the specialized program are still students of the school, but may have limited or no interaction with the rest of the student body. For example, a high school may implement an engineering-based program on campus to which students must apply and be accepted. Students participating in this program will attend school on campus, but their classes, course pathways, and other activities are separate from the remainder of the student body. A school may have several schools within the school or just one. Each of these schools may be designated with its own budget, programming, and administration. In most models, the schools are still identified as one school for state and federal accountability purposes. However, some schools and school districts have extended the model and created an entirely separate school housed on the same campus. In these instances, the school programs are separate and only share the use of the school facilities.

Project-Based Learning

Project-based learning is the instructional practice of assigning projects to students as a means of driving instruction. In project-based learning, students are presented with a problem that must be solved. They are usually assigned to groups or teams for completion of the project. To solve this problem, students have to learn content, usually from more than one content area, and demonstrate mastery of a variety of objectives and skills. The teacher who has assigned the project delivers certain content to students and often provides access to designated resources. Students are responsible for extending their learning and conducting research, using the available resources and the Internet. The project is generally complex and can take as little as a few days to complete, or an entire school semester. With more complex project assignments, teachers expect students to demonstrate mastery of a greater number of learning objectives. Therefore, there may be multiple performance expectations for the project, such as papers, presentations, and more. Some schools integrate project-based learning into the curriculum, while other schools have designed their entire curriculum around project-based learning.

Flipped Classroom Model

A flipped classroom model describes the instructional practice of changing the delivery of instructional content and the opportunities for guided practice within the lesson cycle. In a traditional classroom, a teacher delivers the content and may provide limited guided practice on an in-class assignment. The student may be assigned extended practice independently within the class or in the form of homework. In a flipped classroom model, the student is provided with the instructional content electronically, typically in the form of a recorded lecture or presentation video to watch outside of the classroom. In the classroom, the time that would have been dedicated to delivering content is used to support the student in guided practice. This allows the students more time and access to the teacher during the aspect of the lesson in which they are likely to need the teacher's guidance the most. This practice is considered a flipped classroom because in essence the lesson is done at home and the homework is done at school. Many schools have incorporated flipped lessons into their curriculum sparingly, while other schools have transformed their entire curricular program using the flipped classroom.

Charter Schools

A charter school is a specialized public school that operates according to a charter with a local or national organization. The charter may dictate how the school operates and whom it serves. Charter schools are publicly funded, which means they have to meet state and/or federal accountability standards. However, unlike traditional public schools, charter schools do not obtain funding from local taxes. Attending a charter school is free to students and their parents, but there may be an application or entrance requirements. Charter schools provide communities with additional options for educating their children. Some charter schools specialize in serving at-risk youth, a particular gender, certain career paths, or other niche areas. Proponents of charter schools view these schools as an additional option for students, especially if the community schools are not meeting their needs. However, opponents of charter schools believe that these schools take funding, enrollment, and support away from neighborhood schools.

Middle Colleges

Middle colleges are alternative high school programs that are operated on community campuses. The purpose of a middle college is to provide an alternative environment for high school students and facilitate independent student learning. Students who attend middle colleges are given freedoms and liberty similar to college students and may even have a shorter school day or flexible school schedule. The school is operated by school district staff and students take their traditional high school courses, but they are also given the opportunity to take college-level courses taught by community college professors. Middle colleges often appeal to students who do not fit in with the environment or culture at their traditional school or who seek to earn college course credits while still in high school. Some middle colleges are designed and funded as charter schools while others are developed and operated as part of the traditional public-school system.

Personalized Learning

Personalized learning is the instructional strategy of tailoring academic content and instruction to students based on their individual needs. Personalization can be achieved based on a student's learning styles, personality, interests, career goals, and academic progress. Providing personalized learning can be complex, so much is implemented with computer programs. Before personalization can occur, a student must be assessed on content relative to the type of personalization. For example, if learning will be personalized based on a student's learning style, he or she may take a learning style inventory. Based on the inventory results, a personal learning plan will be developed. The purpose of personalized learning is to address the individual needs of the student, with the goal of helping him or her achieve academic growth and success. Instruction may be differentiated based on the content the student receives, how the content is delivered, how the student is expected to engage with the content, the pace of progress through the content, and how students demonstrate mastery of the content. Personalized learning often accompanies technology implementation models such as one-to-one technology.

Flexible School Day

In a traditional school day, students report to school at a certain time in the morning, remain at school for nearly seven hours, and are then dismissed in the afternoon. A flexible school day modifies this traditional schedule to accommodate students and their families. There are many variations of the flexible school day, which may include attending a four-hour block of school at some scheduled time throughout the day, attending school in the evenings, or attending school at unscheduled times and accumulating hours over the course of a school week. A flexible school day is especially beneficial to students who are at risk of dropping out or have dropped out of school in the past. These students may have personal obligations that make it difficult to attend school on a traditional schedule, such as working full-time or caring for a child. Implementing a flexible school day is beneficial to the school and to students because students can attend school in a way that meets their individual needs and the school can help students complete their academic expectations for accountability purposes.

College and Career Readiness

Dual-Credit Enrollment

Dual-credit enrollment is a curricular program designed to give students the opportunity to earn college credits while they are still in high school. The program is called dual-credit because students enroll in high school and college at the same time. To participate, students must meet entry requirements for the local community college. This usually involves earning a specific score on an exam for math and reading. Once admitted to the college program, students take core courses that earn high school and college credits simultaneously. For example, a student may take a Freshman English 1301 course at the college level, which will also earn credit for the high school English year four requirement. The number of college credits that students may earn depends on the school-college partnership and availability of courses, but many schools offer the opportunity to earn an associate's degree while students are still in high school. This saves students and their families money in college tuition and also increases the likelihood that students will persist in college and earn degrees. These college classes can be taught on the high school campus by a qualified teacher or a visiting professor, or the students may travel to the local community college for part of the school day.

Advance Placement Courses

Advanced placement courses are college-level courses that are taught to high school students. Advanced placement (AP) courses contain the content of college-level courses and are taught with college-level rigor by teachers who meet certain qualifications. These courses are usually core content courses such as reading, math, science, or social studies. Students remain on the high school campus to take these courses and receive high school credit for successful course completion. However, students also have an opportunity to take an exam at the end of each course that can qualify them to earn college credit. If the student achieves an acceptable test score, he or she will earn college credit for that course, which is transferrable to most colleges or universities. Students may participate in a combination of AP and dual-credit courses to increase the number of college credits they can earn while still in high school. This saves students and their families money in college tuition and also increases the likelihood that they will persist in college and earn degrees.

International Baccalaureate Programs

An International Baccalaureate (IB) program is a rigorous school curricular program that has been implemented in schools across the world. In order to participate in this program and to be recognized as an IB school, schools must meet certain program requirements and be monitored and evaluated regularly. The authorization process can take two to three years. As an IB school, schools receive professional development and participate in the international network of IB schools. Additionally, students who attend IB schools often demonstrate higher levels of academic success when compared to schools without IB programs. This is due to the specialized curriculum offered as well as the higher level of rigor in IB schools. Students also have the opportunity to become more culturally aware and sensitive due to their acquisition of a second language as part of the program and their exposure to other students around the world.

Role of Career Pathways in Schools

Career pathways are specific tracks that students can participate in to prepare them for specific career fields or jobs. These tracks or pathways include coursework that is relevant to a student's chosen field. For example, if a student is interested in a career pathway for law and public office, his or her pathway may include more reading, writing, and social studies courses than students in other career pathways, as well as more elective courses related to the skills necessary to be successful in that career. All school levels can implement career pathways. In elementary schools, the delineation between the various pathways may not be as defined as in high schools, but it can lay the foundation for future studies. For example, a student in a fine arts career pathway from elementary school to high school would likely have an advantage over students who did not participate in a career pathway but are interested in fine arts due to the general exposure to and participation in fine arts related coursework. Some state accountability systems require high school students to identify career pathways as part of graduation requirements.

Accountability

Student Growth

Student growth has become a focus in school accountability. In years past, student performance has been the sole focus. As a result, educators primarily focused on students who were likely to perform well on high-stakes tests. As a result, students who were not likely to pass these tests were underserved, along with students who would likely pass the test regardless of teacher intervention and support. In contrast, a focus on student growth and accountability for such growth means that educators must serve all students. Even if a student does not pass a state-mandated test, growth in performance must be demonstrated. This growth is often measured against a prediction of how the student is expected to perform, based on assessment data from previous years. To ensure that schools are adequately educating all students, accountability standards incorporate measures of student growth in addition to measuring student performance.

Student Performance

Student performance in school accountability describes how students perform on state-mandated assessments. A certain percentage of students must pass these tests for a school to be deemed acceptable. This performance is evaluated in each core content area, depending on the accountability system, but most frequently in reading and math. The performance standards and content areas evaluated can vary based on grade level and can also change with federal or state legislature. A school that performs well in one subject and not in another is still a failing school. Additionally, to ensure that all students are performing well and not just certain groups of students, school performance is evaluated for particular subgroups of students, based on demographics. These demographics may include race or ethnicity, socioeconomic status, special education status, limited English proficiency status, and more.

Current Federal Legislation

The most recent legislation related to public school accountability is the Every Student Succeeds Act (ESSA), which was enacted in 2015 during President Obama's administration. This legislation replaced the No Child Left Behind (NCLB) Act of 2002, enacted during President Bush's administration. ESSA provides more flexibility to states by allowing individual states to provide plans for addressing key educational goals such as closing the achievement gap, ensuring and increasing equity in schools, improving the quality of instruction in schools, and improving growth and performance outcomes for all students. However, the basis of the law remains the same as that of NCLB. All students should have full educational opportunity. Consequently, there is a remaining focus on serving low-income students, students with special needs, and other students who have traditionally been marginalized in the public school system.

Consequences for Schools That Do Not Meet Accountability Standards

Schools that do not meet accountability standards may be subject to local, state, or federal sanctions. For a first-time failure, consequences may not be severe. The school will likely have to provide notice to parents and the community that accountability standards were not met. The school may then have to develop a formal plan that outlines changes to help meet accountability standards the following year. Many school districts have strategies and supports in place for schools that do not meet accountability standards. Additionally, the state and federal government provide resources for these schools. The goal is not to punish school staff but to provide the resources and supports necessary to increase the likelihood of student success. This may include training and professional development, consulting staff, curriculum, and more. However, schools that consistently fail to meet accountability standards may experience more severe consequences. These may include changing or removing staff, changing the school leader, implementing specialized or stringent school programming, or even closing the school.

Decreasing Student Dropout Rates

A school's dropout rate is measured for school accountability. Additionally, dropouts miss their educational opportunity. Consequently, many school leaders are developing creative ways to decrease dropout rates. To encourage students to remain in school, leaders are implementing more engaging curricular programs and featuring career pathways and opportunities to earn college credit. Other strategies include providing mentoring programs, offering a variety of extracurricular activities besides sports, and providing counseling and other mental health services. Also, some schools offer accelerated school programming to potential or recovered dropouts in an effort to help them to graduate more quickly. To encourage dropouts to return to school, schools are providing assistance, support, and resources to families. This type of support often requires partnership with other organizations within the community. School leaders and other school staff often visit homes in the community to persuade students who have dropped out to return to school.

Community Leadership

Collaborate with Stakeholders to Use Resources

Engaging Community Stakeholders

A school leader can take several steps to engage community stakeholders in order to utilize community resources and build partnerships. First, the leader should communicate effectively with stakeholders. This communication helps stakeholders to engage because they are aware of the activities happening at the school, the vision and goals for the school, and the accomplishments of the students and staff. When stakeholders are aware of these things, they are able to identify where they can support the school. Next, the school leader should invite stakeholders to visit the school and participate in school activities. This may include activities such as Career Day, awards assemblies, graduation, fairs, and more. Finally, the school leader should engage in activities hosted by community stakeholders. This will demonstrate that the school leader is supportive of their endeavor and is open to learning about the stakeholders' roles in the community. As the leader builds relationships with these stakeholders, he or she can identify individualized ways to further engage community stakeholders.

Supporting School Programs with Community Resources

Almost all aspects of the school program can be supported with community resources. Local community organizations can prove to be valuable in a broad range of areas that benefit the school, its staff, and the students. These may include transportation, training, academic support, extracurricular activities, fundraising, clubs, sponsorships, internships for students, physical resources such as equipment, services, and much more. For example, community volunteers help to maintain school safety with services such as greeting visitors, monitoring halls, or assisting with arrival and dismissal. Some community organizations may be able to provide school supplies for students or classroom supplies for teachers, which can support the instructional program. Other organizations may have access to men and women who can serve as mentors to at-risk youth on campus. It is up to the school leader to identify community resources near the school and determine if and how those resources can benefit the school community.

Benefits of Community Partnerships

Community partnerships are beneficial to the school and the community. Establishing community partnerships is a way of providing resources to students and their families, usually at little or no cost to them. This can be invaluable to low-income families who otherwise would not be able to afford the services. Additionally, establishing community partnerships creates sustainability and stability within the community. When the school and its families patronize the organizations in the community and utilize their services, this helps to ensure that the organization will remain operable in the community. Frequently, services disappear from communities because they are underutilized, especially in impoverished communities. Finally, when the school leader establishes partnerships within the community, this helps to align the school vision and goals with those of the community to garner more support and resources to accomplish the vision and goals.

Variety of Services

Services Provided for Students Through Community Resources

Many community resources used to support schools are targeted toward students in need. Some community resources target academic needs. These include providing tutorial services, free or low-cost school supplies, free books, internships, training programs, and more. Other community resources target physical health needs. These resources may include free or low-cost immunizations, free or low-cost dental services, free or low-cost medical checkups, and more. These types of resources may also address other physical needs of students, such as food, clothing, toiletries, or haircuts and grooming. Additionally, some community resources cater to the psychosocial needs of students. These resources may include mentoring, counseling, therapy, peer mediation, and many others. Some organizations provide specific services while others offer a variety of services. School leaders need to coordinate access to and delivery of these services to best meet students' needs.

Services Provided for Staff Through Community Resources

Even though staff members of the school do not necessarily reside in the community associated with the school, some community organizations extend benefits and resources to staff because of their service to the community. These resources may include memberships or discounts to local business for purchasing food or supplies for the classroom, access to free training or resources that can aid in their professional development, or partnerships with local businesses to supplement instruction in the classroom. Many organizations in the community are willing to donate time, money, or resources and supplies for special events or activities hosted at the school. Consequently, the school leader and staff members should keep community stakeholders informed about school events to help determine how these community partners can support the school.

Services Provided for Parents Through Community Resources

As residents of the community, parents often have access to certain resources. At times, these resources can be delivered through the school to increase the likelihood of parental engagement in these resources. These services may include English as a Second Language (ESL) classes for non-native English speakers, GED or adult high school programs, technology courses, individual and family counseling, and much more. Additionally, some community services assist adults with acquiring housing or meeting household expenses such as rent, utilities, and food. Other services may include childcare, parenting classes, and other supports for the adults and their families. For many of these community organizations, the rationale for providing support to parents is that the children will benefit, which in turn positively affects their school life in areas such as attendance and academic performance.

Value of Partnering with Community and Recreational Centers

When schools partner with community and recreational centers, this is often an opportunity to provide students and their families with resources they may not normally have access to or take advantage of. Often, community members are unaware of services that these organizations provide at little to no cost, such as childcare, use of gym facilities, access to technology, and more. Similarly, these organizations can help to expand the school program. For example, an organization may partner with the school to provide childcare on campus for students whose parents cannot pick them up at school dismissal time. Similarly, a community center may provide GED preparation to adults and can offer these services on the school campus to parents. These partnerships are mutually beneficial and often involve sharing services and facilities.

Collaboration to Benefit Both School and Community

Memorandum of Understanding

A memorandum of understanding is a contract between two parties, outlining the details of an agreement in which no money is exchanged. It is an agreement of services to be provided. For example, an organization may offer to provide tutorial services for students in reading and math after school on campus at no cost to the school. The school and the organization would draft a memorandum of understanding that outlines the tutorial services to be provided and the school leader's promise to provide a location on campus for the services. Both parties would sign the document and receive an original copy. The verbiage of the memorandum of understanding can be the same as in a traditional contract, but often the language is simpler as the sole purpose of the document is to state the exchange of services with no monetary compensation. The purpose of the memorandum of understanding is to document the services that are to be provided. This type of documentation can be helpful for both parties in providing evidence that the services were agreed upon and delivered.

Long-Term Benefits of Collaborating with Community Members

Collaborating with members of the community can have long-term benefits for the school and the surrounding community. When there is collaboration and partnership between the community and the school, there can be an alignment of vision and goals. This fosters long-term, mutually beneficial partnerships. For example, community organizations and the school may identify a need for increased technology education within the community. They can collaborate to add technology programs in the school, programs for adults within the community, and an increase in Internet access for community members. Also, community programs can be integrated into the school program and even housed on the school campus. For example, a GED program may be based on a school campus to increase accessibility to parents and encourage parental engagement at the school. Community support can sustain or boost student enrollment in school and participation in special school programs.

Connection Between the School and Local Employment Trends

The school provides education and training that make students employable in the community workforce. As a result, the school can supplement or adjust programming to respond to community needs, such as training students in particular fields that are experiencing an employment shortage within the community. For example, the school leader and community members may identify a need for more healthcare workers in their community. They can tailor a school program to offer healthcare courses and training that could lead to certifications and degrees in the healthcare field. These students could then enter the local workforce with the skills to fill the needs of local employers. Many schools, especially secondary schools, partner with their local community colleges and community organizations to identify employment trends to support the local community as well as to increase the likelihood that graduates can obtain employment.

Connection Between the School and Local Education Trends

It is beneficial to the school community, the community at large, and postsecondary education institutions to align education expectations between public school and college. Schools and students benefit when there is communication between area colleges and the school for the purpose of understanding the local education trends and needs. For example, the local community college can communicate to school leaders that recently enrolled freshmen have significant deficits in math skills. This information can prompt a school leader to analyze and revise the current math program and make the needed adjustments to ensure that students are graduating with the knowledge and skills needed to be successful in college. Similarly, communication between postsecondary institutions and school leaders can help to identify the soft skills that students need to be successful in college, as well as trends in degree programs and career paths. This type of communication can also lead to the institution of higher education programming on school campuses, such as dual-credit enrollment or training and certification programs.

Benefit of Maintaining a Safe School for the Community

The first priority of a school leader is maintaining school safety. This benefits not only the students and staff, but also the community as a whole. When issues and conflicts identified at the school are resolved promptly, this can prevent escalation of those issues outside the school, which can ultimately prevent violence or other altercations in the community. Also, a safe school in the community becomes a safe haven or refuge for unsafe communities and neighborhoods. Community members are willing to engage in school events when they know that the school is safe and organized. Additionally, community members and organizations are willing to support and invest in schools that are safe and well-run. In contrast, when a school is not safe, this can lead to decreased enrollment and a lack of parental and community support.

Building Relationships with Business, Religious, Political, and Service Organizations

Building Relationships with Various Community Organizations

A school leader can build relationships with various community organizations through effective communication and active participation in community events. First, the school leader should effectively communicate to community leaders that he or she desires to partner and build a relationship. This communication can involve sharing the school vision and goals and learning about the vision and goals of the community organizations. This can lead to a discussion of how the school and community organizations can organize mutually beneficial plans and activities. Collaborating will help to establish relationships. Then, the school leader should be an active participant in community events so that he or she will be visible and recognizable, as well as to show support for the community. This participation may include attending events at other schools in the community, attending church services in the community, or participating in other community-sponsored events. Supporting the activities of community organizations demonstrates investment in the community and helps to build relationships.

Information Sources to Learn About Community Dynamics

It is important for a leader to understand the dynamics of the community to meet the community's needs and to establish productive relationships. These dynamics can be revealed in a variety of ways. Often, community leaders and parents in the community are willing to discuss the community's makeup and dynamics. The school leader can search for publications, such as community newspapers or bulletins, to stay up to date on community affairs. These newspapers often highlight community leaders, organizations, community needs, and upcoming community events. Additionally, the school leader can attend community meetings such as town hall meetings to learn about the concerns of the community. It is also important to learn who the government officials in the area are, as well as candidates running for office in upcoming elections.

Communicating with Families and the Public

Communicating with Families and the Public

A school leader should take advantage of multiple ways of communicating with families and the public. Communication can be facilitated through technology. Methods include emails, electronic newsletters, websites, social media, mass automated phone calls, and other forms of technology that can be used to share messages with large groups of people. The school leader can also communicate in ways that require little or no technology. This includes making personal phone calls, hosting community meetings, making public announcements at community events, mailing letters, and other methods. When hosting community meetings, the leader should ensure that these meetings are held at a variety of times that are convenient for parents and the community, such as early morning, late evening, or weekends. A leader can use a variety of ways to communicate and must identify the most preferred and effective means of communication for the school community. Additionally, the school leader can use multiple modes of communication to share the same message and reach as many people as possible.

Overcoming Language Barriers in Communication

In diverse communities, school leaders often encounter language barriers when attempting to communicate with parents of students or other community members. It is helpful when a leader is fluent in more than one language, but often a variety of languages are spoken in these communities. To overcome language barriers, a leader should be proactive in devising communication strategies. First, the leader should be aware of all languages that are spoken in the school community. Then, the leader should attempt to have school employees who are fluent in the languages spoken on campus so they can translate when needed. Additionally, school communications can be translated into a variety of languages. Translators or translation machines can be available at community meetings, including sign language when appropriate. Many businesses offer translation services for documents, as well as for meetings and conferences held in real time.

Effectively Communicating with the Media

There are times that the school leader will need to communicate effectively with the media, for both positive and negative reasons. The school leader should first follow the protocols and procedures outlined by the school district when communicating with the media, especially in situations in which the media attention is negative for the school or district. Some school districts centralize media communication and do not permit school leaders or other staff to communicate with the media without express approval. When communicating with the media, school leaders should speak truthfully, communicate in alignment with the school and district vision and goals, and communicate according to instructions from the school district staff. A school leader can utilize media outlets to positively highlight the school, such as broadcasting upcoming events or spotlighting student and staff accomplishments.

Formal vs. Informal Communication

Formal communication is usually prepared in advance. The school leader knows what is to be communicated and how. Formal communication is typically structured and controlled and is delivered in a formal way, such as in a presentation to the community or a speech at an event. Formal communication also involves prepared print communication such as a letter, email, or bulletin to the public. In contrast, informal communication is often impromptu. This often involves conversation with an individual or group, an unexpected phone call, or a text message. In informal communication, the topic may be unexpected or vary within the course of communication. Informal communication can occur before or after a formal meeting or event, as a result of an unexpected phone call, or in any variety of circumstances in which the school leader was not prepared for the communication or conversation.

Precautions When Speaking Informally with Stakeholders

A school leader should take precautions when speaking informally with stakeholders to protect self, the school, and the school district. Informal conversation can be used negatively by persons who do not have the best interest of the school or school leader in mind or who are seeking personal gain. As a result, a leader should take care to be professional even in informal speech and to speak in accordance with the school and district vision and goals. For example, a school leader may make a joke during an informal conversation after a parent meeting that the parent does not believe to be in good taste. That parent can then make a formal complaint to the school district regarding the leader's professionalism. Regardless of the leader's perception of his or her relationship with the stakeholder, it is imperative that he or she remembers his or her position as school leader when engaging in informal conversation. The leader should view all communication, formal or informal, as a reflection of the position of school leader and of the school and school district.

Best Practices for Communicating Through Email

When communicating via email, a school leader should make sure that the email communicates the message in the intended way. In order to do this, the leader should maintain a professional tone. Humor and sarcasm are not often conveyed well via email and should be avoided. The school leader should also review the email for proper spelling, grammar, and word use, as errors can cause the message to be misunderstood. The leader should use features such as *Reply All* and *cc* with caution, only sending the email to persons who need to be included in the conversation. Also, the school leader should confirm that any necessary attachments are included in the email, if applicable. It is also a good practice to confirm with the recipient that the email has been received. Emails with attachments or mass emails are sometimes redirected to the recipient's spam or junk mail folder and may not be received in a timely manner, if at all.

Considerations When Scheduling Parent Meetings

When scheduling parent meetings for large groups of parents, the school leader should consider the time of day and day of the week that these meetings are to be held. The goal of these meetings is to effectively communicate with parents in a group setting, so the school leader needs to ensure that the scheduled day and time accommodate the majority of parents for maximum attendance. The ideal times for these events will vary based on the needs of parents in the community. In many communities, parents work during the day, so evening meetings are more favorable. In some communities, certain days of the week are dedicated to religious activities, sporting events, or other engagements, and this should be taken into consideration when scheduling a parent meeting. For example, a school leader would not want to schedule a parent meeting at the elementary school on the same evening as the high school football game, as this would put the two events in competition. The school leader can talk to parents and survey families to identify ideal times to host meetings and should be open to hosting meetings at a variety of times, such as early in the morning or on weekends.

Involving Families in Decision Making

Shared Decision-Making Committee

The purpose of the Shared Decision-Making Committee (SDMC) in schools is to provide a structured process for the inclusion of stakeholders in the school decision-making process. This committee is made up of school leadership, school staff, parents, community members, and other key stakeholders that the school leader may choose to include. The committee meets regularly to discuss key decisions that the school leader will make. These decisions may involve school programming, fundraising, planning for school events, and other initiatives. In these meetings, participants are informed of key details that should be considered in making these decisions and are given the opportunity to voice their opinions on the decisions as well as to provide recommendations. The SDMC provides recommendations to the school leader but does not have authority to dictate decisions. However, the SDMC provides an opportunity for stakeholder participation in the school process and helps to build relationships between the school leader and stakeholders.

Ways for Families to Be Involved in School Decision-Making

The school leader should provide as many opportunities as possible to include families in school decision-making. First, the leader should inform families in advance of decisions that will be made. For example, the leader may alert the parents that he or she is considering converting the school playground into a garden. This gives families an opportunity to provide feedback prior to the decision. The school leader can use surveys to gather input from families regarding the school, providing data that can be used in decision-making. Additionally, the school leader can communicate with parent organizations on campus or form a parent focus group to gather feedback and opinions on decisions to be made at the school. Also, there should always be at least one parent representative on the Shared Decision-Making Committee.

Ways for Families to Be Involved in the Decisions Made About Their Child's Education

Each family should have the opportunity to be involved in decisions made about their individual child's education. These decisions may include course selection or school programming pathways, extracurricular activities like clubs and sports, opportunities for tutorials and extended learning, and many others. First, the school should provide clear and effective communication to the families, indicating areas of the school program in which they can help make decisions for their children. Then, the school leader can provide ways for parents to offer their opinions, such as through frequent parent meetings or holding one-on-one conferences. Also, phone calls and emails can be very effective in including parents in the decision-making process. Many schools send informative letters or bulletins home to parents to include them in the process. Some campuses have opted to staff a parent liaison who specializes in communicating with parents and encouraging their participation in the school decision-making process.

Benefits of Involving Families in Decision-Making

Involving families in decision-making is beneficial to both the families and the school. When families are involved in the process, this increases buy-in for the decisions that are made, which can lead to increased support for school initiatives. For example, if families help to decide which tutoring program to implement after school, they will be more likely to have their child participate in the tutorials. Involving families in decision-making also strengthens the relationship between the school and families and stimulates parental engagement. Also, when families are involved, they often share information and a perspective that can inform the school leader's decisions. This can help the leader make decisions that better address the needs of students and their families.

Need for Two-Way Communication

Two-way communication is the process of sending and receiving messages. In two-way communication, a person who receives a message has an opportunity to respond or send a message back to the sender. When collaborating with stakeholders and families, it is important for the school leader to provide opportunities for two-way communication, in contrast to only sending one-way messages. Two-way communication helps the leader to confirm that the message or communication was received as intended. Sometimes a message can be unclear or misinterpreted, and this confusion can be identified in two-way communication. Additionally, two-way communication allows the school leader to learn more about the opinions, needs, and concerns of key stakeholders. Finally, two-way communication promotes involvement and engagement of the stakeholders, which can foster relationships between them and the school and increase buy-in from the stakeholders in regard to the school leader's vision and goals.

Ensuring Two-Way Communication

A leader can ensure two-way communication by providing many opportunities for stakeholders to communicate with him or her. For example, a school leader may host a community meeting and provide a time during the program for stakeholders to ask questions or voice their opinions. School leaders can also make themselves accessible to those seeking to communicate with them. This can be done in several ways, such as holding frequent meetings with stakeholders or choosing certain office hours with an "open-door policy." Other ways of promoting communication include sending out surveys, creating a comment or feedback box on campus, and being open to phone calls and emails. A school leader should be visible during parent and community events and display a willingness to engage in conversation with stakeholders, demonstrating receptiveness to two-way communication.

CPACE Practice Test

Answer Questions 1 through 3 based on the following description:

> A school leader has been hired as the new principal of a public elementary school. State standardized test scores in English Language Arts (ELA) across all fourth-grade classes in this school have steadily declined over the past several years. Scores in reading, listening, and speaking have all declined, and scores in writing started out the lowest and have dropped the most since. The new principal and all fourth-grade teachers are meeting to study samples of student compositions and discuss how to improve writing achievement.

1. The teachers have each brought writing samples from their students to the meeting. The principal should advise them to take which of these steps first toward instructional improvements?

    a. Use the samples to identify students needing remedial instruction.
    b. Perform an analysis of all writing samples, and give scores to each.
    c. Review all of the writing samples and identify and group student needs.
    d. Identify samples for use as benchmark examples next school year.

2. Following the initial meeting, the new principal conducts observations of each fourth-grade teacher's classroom instruction. What should the principal mainly focus on in terms of improving students' state standardized ELA test scores?

    a. Whether teachers are aligning lesson objectives with state grade-level ELA standards
    b. Whether teachers are incorporating instructional strategies for diverse student needs
    c. Whether teachers are implementing their lesson plans as written in classroom activities
    d. Whether teachers are aligning lesson objectives with materials and teaching strategies

3. The principal wants to assist the teachers in identifying the best instructional strategies to augment their students' ELA achievement. Which of the following pairs of data sets would most inform this assistance?

    a. Fourth-grade students' reading levels; fourth-grade ELA instructional schedules
    b. Demographic information on the students; the vision statement for the school
    c. Fourth-grade teachers' years of experience; fourth-grade teachers' educations
    d. Student standardized test data, disaggregated; state grade-level ELA standards

4. A principal wants to develop a new school vision and goals associated with that vision. What applies most about implementing these?

    a. The principal must ensure that the vision and associated goals are all measurable for every student.
    b. The principal must differentiate measurable versus nonmeasurable vision and goals for every student.
    c. The principal must ensure vision and goals, rather than expectations are measurable, for all students.
    d. The principal must develop vision and goals, and school staff must develop an implementation plan.

5. Regarding a school's vision, mission, and related goals, the school leader's responsibility is to ensure these are congruent with which level(s) of education policy?

a. With only the school and district policies
b. With the school, district, and state policies
c. With only federal and state-level policies
d. With school, local, state, and federal policies

6. A school leader surveys key stakeholders regarding the school vision and goals to learn what they believe about the purposes of education. Which set of stakeholder groups is the leader LEAST likely to survey about this particular topic?

a. Superintendent, central office administrators
b. Members of school board, parents of students
c. Community business owners, business workers
d. Students, teachers, paraprofessionals at school

7. To gather feedback from key stakeholders about the relationship between their opinions about the significance of education and the school's vision and goals, which of these should a school leader do?

a. Develop a series of critical questions appropriate to this topic.
b. Develop a few open-ended questions to stimulate discussions.
c. Develop a school task force to interview all of the stakeholders.
d. Develop a series of meetings wherein stakeholders discuss this.

8. To implement the school vision and pursue the school goals, how should a school leader best invite others to share these commitments?

a. Identify only members of the school staff with common perspectives to ensure cooperation.
b. Identify members of school and community with common perspectives to attain consensus.
c. Identify school and community members with diverse perspectives to assure representation.
d. Identify only members of the school staff with diverse perspectives to implement equitably.

9. What does research show about school leaders distributing leadership responsibilities for implementing a school vision and goals?

a. The most effective leaders are found to influence student achievement and school efficacy directly.
b. Today's schools cannot be led by one principal without significant participation by other educators.
c. The traditional model of single, formal leadership exists because teachers lack a principal's expertise.
d. Educational programs developed by one principal are easier for principals who follow to maintain.

10. As part of an overall school reform initiative, a principal makes a plan to distribute leadership among educators and other stakeholders for implementing school goals. Which research findings exist to inform this decision?

a. Distributing leadership improves professional development but nothing else.
b. Educational reform changes demand efforts requiring a few superior leaders.
c. The capacity building needed for school improvement limits leader numbers.
d. School reform initiatives all share implicit distributed leadership in common.

11. Which statement is MOST accurate and complete regarding school leader skills for promoting staff communication and collaboration in problem solving toward school improvement and reform to realize school vision and goals?

a. School leaders communicate school vision and goals to stakeholders, which suffices.
b. School leaders evaluate staff leadership abilities and select those with the best skills.
c. School leaders use consensus building and group-process skills in facilitating reform.
d. School leaders evaluate staff collaborative skills and select those with the best skills.

12. To assess and monitor progress toward school goals, which type(s) of assessment would be MOST indicated for measuring student analytical and critical thinking and communication skills?

a. Performance assessments, journals
b. Standardized tests of achievement
c. Extended student group projects
d. Teacher's observations of students

13. Which of the following is the MOST effective strategy for a principal to communicate the school vision to school personnel?

a. Morning announcements
b. Sending a daily e-mail to staff
c. Attending community events
d. Meetings in one-way format

14. For a school principal to assess the effectiveness of his or her strategies to communicate the school vision, which method would be MOST informative?

a. Separately ask a group of students and a group of parents what the vision is; see if answers align.
b. Separately ask the teachers and a group of parents to state the vision, and compare their answers.
c. Separately ask different members of the school staff to articulate the vision, comparing responses.
d. Separately ask an educational leader, student, teacher, and parent the vision; see if answers align.

15. A principal forms and helps train a school vision oversight team before involving the whole faculty in developing a school vision statement. What best describes the primary purpose of this team?

a. To draft the vision because most school faculties are too big to be productively involved
b. To introduce the concept, engage faculty in writing a vision, and synthesize all their input
c. To represent the school leadership team on a smaller level by delegating some members
d. To represent all school department staff, including those who are not already educational leaders

16. School leadership experts have observed that many available forms of school data can be more significant for informing and guiding the school vision than the kinds of data educators tend to think of automatically. Which choice represents this default assumption that can exclude other valuable data?

a. Standardized achievement, state, local common, AP, and IB test results
b. Data that measure rates of student attendance, absence, and tardiness
c. Rates of attendance, absence, and turnover of grade or department staffs
d. Student extracurricular enrollments and incidents and dispositions in discipline

17. To address inherent barriers like staff fear of the unknown and resistance to change, school principals benefit from knowing common kinds of inner dialogues employees experience around school vision development for listening to and validating their thoughts. What do school personnel typically ask themselves about this change process?

a. Not what is needed for the vision but if they will be able to live with and support it
b. If they believe they and the school can realize the vision rather than if they believe in it
c. Whether they will be able to continue their instructional practices along with why or why not
d. What the vision will expect and how their lives will change more than practice continuity

18. A principal has assembled a school vision oversight team and provided them with a variety of school data for background knowledge. The team is ready to engage school staff in developing a new school vision. Faculty members review the current vision statement, examples of others' vision statements, and school data. The team divides staff into groups with discussion questions; for example, "What kind of school do we aspire to be?" What other question would apply?

a. "How is our school just the same as any other school?"
b. "What do we think our vision statement should reflect?"
c. "What should we keep on doing to realize this vision?"
d. "What is evidence we are meeting the current vision?"

19. Relative to developing and sustaining a clear school vision and learning goals, which choice correctly describes documented practices of effective school principals?

a. They protect educators' instructional time via minimizing disruptions.
b. They set aspirational goals that they do not expect everyone to meet.
c. They have a clear vision for the school and always focus on one vision.
d. They ensure continual progress monitoring regardless of school goals.

20. The research literature about school principals' roles in realizing the school vision and goals, and aligning instruction with the vision and goals, affords which of these conclusions?

a. Principals with more effective schools focus on learning rather than on school improvement.
b. Principals with high-achieving schools have more confidence in teachers than in themselves.
c. Principals with effective schools delegate the roles of assuring instructional quality to others.
d. Principals with high-achieving schools communicate to all stakeholders that learning comes first.

21. To create a culture of high expectations for students, some school leaders and teachers have instituted "no zeroes" grading policies wherein students received progressive interventions and new due dates to achieve at least 70% on assignments instead of 0% the first time. What best reflects student outcomes?

a. Far fewer students received F grades.
b. Missed assignments remained equal.
c. More students received a D grade.
d. More students received extra help.

22. Research into achievement gaps in suburban schools known for excellence found which of the following about students from racial and ethnic minority groups?

a. Black and Latino students spent less time on homework and completed homework less.
b. Researchers attributed differences in grades and homework to motivation and effort.
c. Asian students had higher grades and finished more homework by spending equal time.
d. Researchers attributed grade and homework differences to skill and home support gaps.

23. The Tripod Project and other research-based initiatives to close achievement gaps have identified aspects of student engagement. For example, when teachers help them consolidate new learning, students are prepared for the future. Among other aspects, each described here as opposing pairs leading to success or failure, which is incorrect?

a. Trust and interest versus mistrust and disinterest
b. Autonomy of students versus control by teachers
c. Ambition in learning versus. ambivalence toward it
d. Industry versus disengagement or discouragement

24. Among guidelines for school leaders to embed standards-based professional development (PD) into teachers' jobs, which pair is described accurately?

a. Effective PD is student centered; teachers are actively involved in learning processes.
b. Job-embedded and school-based PD is on-site; teachers independently problem solve.
c. PD is supported and ongoing; teachers must know practical applications, not theories.
d. PD is part of district-supported systematic reform; it must cover new, unstudied trends.

25. In steps for school leaders to take to develop professional learning communities for identifying instructional practices to augment student learning, the first is that school leaders and faculty endorse the school purpose of high-level learning for every student. Which of the other steps is represented correctly here?

a. School leaders form staff teams whose members collaborate in accomplishing diverse goals.
b. School leaders assign teams to develop, not administer, assessments nor design curriculum.
c. School leaders and staff teams identify both exemplary and struggling teachers and students.
d. School leaders let staff teams develop coordinated intervention plans but do not participate.

26. The National PTA identifies factors promoting family school involvement as a critical form of stakeholder collaboration. Which factor(s) is/are more the responsibility of school leaders than the collective responsibility of school leaders, faculty, and staff?

a. Supporting the parenting skills of the parents or guardians of the students
b. Actively participating in and encouraging parental involvement in student learning
c. Engaging students' parents to become partners for school decision making
d. Community outreach, encouraging family volunteers, and serving on PTAs

27. A school leader is new to the community and attends a district school board meeting. In what way can attending this meeting best support the development of this school leader's beliefs about educational issues?

a. By displaying the diverse issues and viewpoints across the unfamiliar school district
b. By demonstrating the areas of disagreement within a school district
c. By allowing the school leader the opportunity to learn how to run school board meetings
d. By shedding light on differences between a school's vision and the district vision

28. As school leader responsibilities have increased, distributing leadership has become more important. Distributive leadership can have additive or holistic forms. Which of the following is correct regarding these forms?

a. In the additive form, collective work by all leaders adds up to more than the sum of its parts.
b. In the holistic form, every organizational member is a leader, regardless of his or her interactions.
c. In the additive form, all organizational leaders must "sink or swim" together, not separately.
d. In the holistic form, interdependent leadership among organization members is emphasized.

29. Regarding how school leaders involve students appropriately in school improvement teams and processes, which of the following is true?

a. Planning school-wide forums is always a school leader's job.
b. Some students have conducted school-wide survey research.
c. Students have never participated in hiring any school leader.
d. Students testifying in the state legislatures is against the law.

30. Which of the following things can school leaders do to give teachers a safe environment for expressing their ideas?

a. Giving critical feedback about unusual ideas they express
b. Scheduling regular, brief meeting times for original ideas
c. Taking care not to let teachers undermine their authority
d. Asking them how "safe" differs for teachers versus students

31. What have researchers found about the roles of school leaders relative to teacher risk taking?

a. Principals who follow traditional authoritarian approaches receive more respect from teachers.
b. When principals allow more freedom in curriculum design, teachers miss their leaders' control.
c. Teachers attribute their success to empowerment by principals who give freedom to take risks.
d. Researchers find that to meet student needs, school leaders must minimize teacher risk taking.

32. Regarding strategies that principals can use to give teachers effective feedback, which is true?

a. Principals will make feedback fresher for teachers by delivering it unexpectedly.
b. Principals should give feedback unrelated to their expectations or teacher goals.
c. Principals enable perspective by delaying feedback after classroom observation.
d. Principals convey criticism best following strengths and by requesting solutions.

33. Educational research into collaborative data analysis has identified four areas. Which of these areas involves the process of exploring learning standards, goals, and definitions?

a. Calibration
b. Student data focus
c. Educator engagement
d. Supportive technology

34. Among standards informing effective professional development (PD) for teachers, which is/are most characteristic of strong school leaders?

a. Valuing ongoing learning, promoting continuous improvement, and inquiry, collaboration, and problem-solving
b. Realizing good PD's value, promoting teacher participation, and communicating PD benefits to stakeholders
c. Human, financial, and temporal contributions; allocation coordination; and investment return assessments
d. Rigorous analysis of varied, disaggregated student data for proficiency standards, learning gaps, and results

35. Which of these is NOT one of the purposes of rigorous and relevant curriculum design?

a. To challenge educator views on how students learn
b. To incorporate the instructional skills of the teacher
c. To impose a structure on existing instructional goals
d. To incorporate new and different instructional goals

36. Among tenets of the philosophy of differentiating instruction that are compatible with standards-based instruction, which is described correctly here?

a. The Zone of Proximal Development enables optimal learning.
b. Designed learning opportunities are superior to natural ones.
c. Activating prior knowledge enhances relevance, not learning.
d. Sense of community aids social, not academic, development.

37. A high school teacher's Algebra II class includes some students learning independently, some progressing as fast as she could teach them, and some lacking prerequisite skills for the course. The teacher's dual goal is to help every student acquire a solid grasp of mathematics and also pass the standards exam. Which of the following practices help her achieve this?

a. Letting students discover curriculum skills to master instead of telling them
b. Devoting most small-group instruction time to students needing more help
c. Dividing classroom time among varied instructional groupings and activities
d. Focusing on introducing new concepts rather than prior student knowledge

38. Regarding data collection, recording, and submission for monitoring student progress and relating it to state assessments, which school leader responsibility to help faculty is MOST accurately described?

a. Deciding how often, and to whom, teachers submit data
b. Ensuring teachers collect data periodically, for example, quarterly
c. Having faculty aid one another with data-recording forms
d. Applying state-assigned rubrics to assessment for faculty

39. How must school leaders help faculty and other staff with curriculum and instruction to identify and meet student needs?

a. They oversee but do not participate in designing curriculum and instruction.
b. They review programs regularly to determine correct implementation only.
c. They help faculty and staff meet unmet needs rather than implement plans.
d. They help faculty and staff identify content and practices to address needs.

40. When school principals collaborate with others in making curriculum decisions, who else should be involved?

a. Curriculum specialists and professional personnel
b. Curriculum specialists, professionals, and board members
c. The students and the school's professional personnel
d. School professionals and members of the board of education

41. What best describes knowledge of instructional practices that school leaders must have?

a. Helping teachers learn new methods but not predicting how long it will take
b. Knowing the time effective planning takes regardless of the number of students
c. Implementing new approaches, more importantly than networking teachers
d. Knowing the time effective planning takes according to the levels of content

42. Which of the following applies to both horizontal and vertical curriculum alignment?

a. Teaching the same content across all classrooms on the same grade levels
b. Teaching content aligned with state or district assessments and standards
c. Teaching to minimize achievement gaps through standardizing education
d. Teaching across successive grade levels including preparatory scaffolding

43. School leaders should regularly review and analyze teachers' learning objectives, assessments, progress, and achievement data collection and use their analyses to determine which of the following?

a. How well these elements align with one another within and across grade levels and curriculum
b. How well these elements align with state or national standards rather than with one another
c. How well these elements align with one another within grade levels rather than across levels
d. How well these elements align with one another across grade levels instead of the curriculum

44. To assist teachers with integrating technology into instruction, which should school leaders do?

a. Lead teachers first to encourage student technology use for enhancing research skills
b. Lead teachers to avoid legal and ethical issues with technology as outside their scope
c. Lead teachers to encourage student concept comprehension before using technology
d. Lead teachers to target technology skills and content quality without differentiation

45. School leaders can organize teachers into data inquiry teams to identify and address student academic needs. What accurately describes something school leaders should direct these teams to do?

a. Develop action plans according to data analyses.
b. Support the implementation of the action plans.
c. Analyze data from summative assessments only.
d. Analyze data by classes, not individual students.

46. What best reflects research findings about factors influencing school achievement gaps?

a. School curriculum and resources correlate with student achievement more strongly than socioeconomic status (SES).
b. SES correlates more strongly with achievement than school resources.
c. Student SES correlates more strongly with student achievement than school curriculum does.
d. Student achievement correlates more strongly with SES and school resources than curriculum.

47. Which of these is recommended for school leaders to plan classroom visits effectively for giving teachers useful observational feedback?

a. Completing a checklist during every classroom visit
b. Giving teachers individual, not collective, feedback
c. Making walk-throughs to give summative feedback
d. Using statistics to give individual teacher feedback

48. Experts advise school leaders to create a clear vision for the best use of school-wide student achievement data and to communicate this vision. What else do they recommend for using these data?

a. School leaders should institute supports to develop a data-driven school culture.
b. School leaders should instruct faculty, not students, to understand and use data.
c. School leaders should develop and maintain data systems specific to the school.
d. School leaders should separate data from the cycle of continuous improvement.

49. School leaders can institute consistent, routine, effective data-based decision making by establishing strong school cultures for data use through forming a school-wide data team. What should this team do?

a. Hold the staff accountable for data use.
b. Supervise a school staff's data activities.
c. Lead school staff by modeling data use.
d. Provide school staff with expert advice.

50. Among classroom assessment principles that school leaders must know for effective collaboration with teachers, which choice is MOST representative?

a. A few specific assessment instruments are error free.
b. Authors and users typically overestimate testing error.
c. Assessment reliability applies to tests, not test scores.
d. Good assessment is valid, reliable, ethical, and fair.

51. Among school leader responsibilities for managing daily school facility operations, which is MOST likely to involve district support for hiring expert consultants to address contemporary issues?

a. Managing the food services in the school
b. Managing school environmental quality
c. Managing school transportation services
d. Managing custodial services in a school

52. Regarding school buildings and grounds maintenance, for which of these are school leaders directly responsible?

a. Inspection and maintenance procedure development
b. Allocation of budget for inspection and maintenance
c. Inspection and maintenance schedules development
d. Preventive maintenance procedures implementation

53. Leadership is one of the factors identified by research as instrumental in implementing school-wide technology adoption. This includes multiple roles for school leaders. Which set of responsibilities is associated with the role of learning organization leader?

a. Making change a priority, supporting and encouraging teacher endeavors
b. Making sure that teachers have what they need to meet goals for change
c. Setting high learning and collaborative standards as conditions for change
d. Leading initiatives, resolving problems, and providing learning opportunities for faculty

54. In a school's Acceptable Use Policy (AUP) for classroom Internet technology, which section is MOST likely to cross-reference or even duplicate the general school disciplinary code?

a. Violations and sanctions
b. Acceptable uses
c. Unacceptable uses
d. Policy statement

55. What is MOST true about how school district personnel and school leaders plan school budgets?

a. They can predict employee benefits expenses more easily than salaries.
b. Estimating next year's budget expenses excludes any emergency funds.
c. Districts issue school budgets for leaders without enrollment numbers.
d. School budgets omit necessary and costly expenses for transportation.

56. Researchers have identified which essential findings about how school leaders recruit, assign, develop, and retain highly qualified teachers?

a. Effective schools avoid hiring good teachers from other schools.
b. Effective schools assign new teachers preferentially to students.
c. Effective schools improve teachers more but at the same speed.
d. Effective schools retain superior faculty more than other schools.

57. To develop staff leadership skills that advance the school vision, which activities that school leaders can ask staff members to participate in fall into the category of helping staff increase their skill and knowledge bases?

a. Serve on school leadership teams, lead faculty study groups, help on school improvement projects, and lead curriculum planning committees.
b. Help screen and interview job applicants, attend district meetings, work on less familiar projects, and help others work with challenging parents.
c. Discuss reasons and ways that school leaders handled situations as opportunities to observe and reflect, and journal leader practice observations.
d. Join and participate in professional organizations, mentor new employees, and present information to other members of the school staff.

58. Related to school safety plans, goals for school leaders include which of these?

a. Leading school needs assessments, safety plan development, and implementation monitoring
b. Developing a system to monitor school incidents and crime that others share with stakeholders
c. Appointing personnel to design safe traffic patterns inside and outside the school environment
d. Adopting emergency evacuation procedures and delegating crisis management procedure choices

59. Developing a school safety plan requires the participation of which of the following and for which reason?

a. School leaders and staff, because only they know their school and students best
b. School personnel only, because schools are for controlling as well as for learning
c. The entire community, because school crime data reflect community crime data
d. Law enforcement and mental health professionals, because they address crimes

60. Among challenges that school leaders face in their efforts to promote student mental health, which of the following descriptions most represents the category of limited resources?

a. Accountability law has shifted school counselors' duties from mental health to academic achievement.
b. Prevention and promotion can address most student issues, yet costly treatments are routinely prescribed.
c. The mental health resources available to public schools are not provided proportionately or equitably.
d. Owing to our society's cultural traditions, the priority of mental health issues in schools is marginalized.

61. Which category of mental health obstacles to student learning and achievement includes the LEAST proportion of factors that can arise in and be addressed in schools?

a. External stressors
b. Educational problems
c. Psychosocial problems
d. Psychological disorders

62. The National Association of Secondary School Principals (NASSP) recommends that school leaders furnish comprehensive staff development in supporting student mental health. Which area of recommended training is most related to the Response to Intervention (RtI) model?

a. Early identification of students having or at risk of mental disorders
b. The use of referral mechanisms for school and community services
c. Strategies to apply in promoting school-wide positive environments
d. Models for consultation, coordination, and collaboration in schools

63. Among responsibilities of the school leader related to the school emergency plan are to conduct emergency response drills, evaluate staff responses, and revise the plan based on the results. These activities apply to which phase of emergency management?

a. Preparedness
b. Prevention
c. Response
d. Recovery

64. The U.S. Department of Homeland Security has adopted the National Incident Management System (NIMS) for all federal, state, and local government agencies in emergency response. This system includes the Incident Command System (ICS). School district and building emergency response teams are organized based on ICS management functions. Which of these functions develops incident response objectives?

a. Planning
b. Logistics
c. Command
d. Operations

65. What is true about school leader responsibilities for documentation related to school safety?

a. They must communicate rather than document implementation monitoring feedback.
b. They must document their observations from monitoring safety plan implementation.
c. They must document school safety incidents but not related feedback to stakeholders.
d. They must not allow others to document the safety management procedures they adopt.

66. Regarding school collaboration with key stakeholders to eliminate barriers to learning, which of the following is a valid reason for such collaboration related to mental health services?

a. Most school-age children in the United States have several options for mental health services.
b. Services like clinical psychiatric care are unfeasible and inappropriate in the schools.
c. Students and parents are more comfortable with familiar school settings and staffs.
d. Research studies find students are less likely to seek counseling services in schools.

67. Which statement is true with respect to segregated educational services for individual student needs and integrated comprehensive educational services?

a. Students benefit more from specific educator expertise through segregated than integrated services.
b. A principle of service integration is student centeredness, that is, targeting the student as a failure source.
c. Educators should design their curriculum and instruction beginning with appropriate differentiation.
d. Educators should develop curriculum for average students and then adapt it for individual students.

68. Regarding family involvement in educational decision making for their children, which of these statements is LEAST accurate?

a. Families are important to collaboration as their children's primary advocates.
b. Families are inspired to participate by the minority of families who volunteer.
c. Families can advocate for other families as aspects of school-based dialogues.
d. Families can provide service and support in developing learning communities.

69. Some successful school leaders have obtained public and financial support for their schools by communicating with community members. Which example of this is most applicable?

a. Sharing real estate data with the business community is unrelated to school success.
b. Local families are drawn to schools more by physical changes than better test scores.
c. Significant improvements for minority students are best shared within the first year.
d. Leaders should share substantial, overall school academic gains with families yearly.

70. School leaders and schools realize benefits from engaging community partners. Which of the following such benefits contribute(s) MOST to successful student interactions in the wider world beyond their immediate community?

a. Greater social capital through relationships
b. Access to needed health and social services
c. Safe opportunities to experiment and lead
d. Adult guidance and positive role modeling

71. School leaders are finding that communicating with the media helps them engage the public in education. Researchers find this public engagement reinforces community pride. What else do they find it does?

a. It has no effects upon local safety or security.
b. It increases public criticism of school reforms.
c. It helps the schools rather than communities.
d. It increases service to the school and community.

72. A constructivist model for evaluating educational programs incorporates multiple stakeholder perspectives. Which of the following correctly sequences the steps for school leaders and others to follow in this approach?

a. Discover stakeholder concerns, issues, and assertions; furnish a method and context for collecting and analyzing stakeholder feedback; identify stakeholders; establish a forum enabling negotiation; gather and disseminate information for negotiating; use an agenda for negotiations; reach consensus within and among stakeholder groups; review any unresolved matters; and make and deliver a report to stakeholders.
b. Identify stakeholders; discover stakeholder concerns, issues, and assertions; furnish a method and context for collecting and analyzing stakeholder feedback; reach consensus within and among stakeholder groups; use an agenda for negotiations; gather and disseminate information for negotiating; establish a forum enabling negotiation; make and deliver a report to stakeholders; and review any unresolved matters.
c. Establish a forum enabling negotiation; gather and disseminate information for negotiating; use an agenda for negotiations; reach consensus within and among stakeholder groups; discover stakeholder concerns, issues, and assertions; identify stakeholders; review any unresolved matters; make and deliver a report to stakeholders; and furnish a method and context for collecting and analyzing stakeholder feedback.
d. Furnish a method and context for collecting and analyzing stakeholder feedback; identify stakeholders; establish a forum enabling negotiation; discover stakeholder concerns, issues, and assertions; gather and disseminate information for negotiating; reach consensus within and among stakeholder groups; review any unresolved matters; make and deliver a report to stakeholders; and use an agenda for negotiations.

73. Measures of the effects of school community engagement strategies include changes in the behaviors and attitudes of parents, families, community members, and students. What represents some of these impacts on students?

a. Greater school achievement and fewer school behavior problems
b. Greater school attendance in spite of the same school enrollment
c. Greater school enrollment but not necessarily school achievement
d. Greater school achievement, although not necessarily satisfaction

74. When school leaders have engaged communities and families in school reform initiatives, what have they found about the responses of parents, families, and community members?

a. Parents attended more school events and meetings than school trainings.
b. School-to-family outreach would not engender family-to-school outreach.
c. More parents became advocates and organizers for school improvement.
d. Community members served on school councils more than parents would.

75. School leaders need to access multiple information sources to understand and address diverse student and community dynamics. As one type of source, their state education departments can share leadership and accountability and support school leaders. Which example of this helps school leaders in their jobs by facilitating their analyses of school strengths, needs, progress, and trends?

a. Establishing online networks and electronic LISTSERVs for them
b. Strengthening resources and refining data collection methods
c. Organizing conferences designed especially for school leaders
d. Initiating mentoring and coaching programs for school leaders

76. To engage diverse family and community members, school leaders and staff must make efforts to bridge gaps in language, culture, literacy, education, and so on. Which strategy MOST addresses cultural differences?

a. Having multilingual staff interpret at meetings, trainings, school events, and home visits
b. Suggesting parents ask children about assignments rather than help with homework
c. Assigning parent and community rooms for teacher and other parent meetings and information
d. Hiring community liaisons to help staff understand parental beliefs about education

77. Which choice best describes one of the benefits of collaborations among schools, community agencies, resources, organizations, universities, and businesses?

a. They can coordinate among discrete visions and missions.
b. They can share some resources but cannot pool funding.
c. They can offer multiple services within the school setting.
d. They can share little information because of privacy laws.

78. In seeking community support and additional resources, how do effective school leaders communicate with prospective partners?

a. Define how school leaders' needs and stakeholders' wants can coincide.
b. Speak reactive language when communicating with business executives.
c. Identify business or organization visions exactly matching school visions.
d. To motivate them, explain to partner prospects how schools will benefit.

79. To communicate information to prospective community partners about resources they have and those they need, which approach that school leaders have found effective for motivating community leader engagement is MOST based on evoking intellectually and emotionally meaningful connections?

a. Simply asking prospective partners to listen to what they say
b. Asking how education experiences shaped who they are now
c. Sharing the story of their school with the community leaders
d. Clearly identifying their school's assets and its greatest needs

80. The Institute for Educational Leadership defines some fundamental "rules of engagement" for developing and maintaining school-community partnerships using this mnemonic: "Find out, Reach out, Spell out, Work out," and "Build out." For example, "Find out" refers to discovering each other's needs and interests. Which of the others refers to sharing success and supporting greater endeavors?

a. "Build out"
b. "Spell out"
c. "Work out"
d. "Reach out"

81. The National Association of Secondary School Principals (NASSP) recommendations for ethical behaviors by school leaders include the following:

1. Fulfilling their professional duties honestly and with integrity
2. Obeying all the federal, state, and local laws and regulations
3. Basing all decisions on the value of student success and well-being
4. Acting to change laws, policies and regulations against education goals
5. Implementing the local board of education regulations and policies

Which combination of these could MOST present a conflict for a school leader in some instances?

a. I and III
b. II and IV
c. II, IV, and V
d. III, IV, and V

82. The American Association of School Administrators (AASA) Code of Ethics and the National Association of Secondary School Principals (NASSP) recommendations for a code of ethical conduct for school leaders share many items in common. Which of the following standards does the AASA include that the NASSP recommendations do not?

a. Not using positions for personal gain through political, economic, social, religious, or other influences
b. Only accepting academic degrees or professional certifications from institutions that are accredited
c. Sustaining standards and improving the profession's efficacy with research and professional development
d. Accepting responsibility and accountability for their actions and committing to serve others over self

83. Under the National Education Association (NEA) Code of Ethics, Principle I, Commitment to the Student, educators are enjoined against doing a number of things, including that they: "[s]hall not disclose information about students obtained in the course of professional service unless disclosure serves a compelling professional purpose or is required by law." This reflects which of the following federal laws?

a. The Civil Rights Act of 1964
b. The Family Educational Rights and Privacy Act (FERPA) and/or the Individuals with Disabilities Act (IDEA)
c. Americans with Disabilities Act (ADA) Amendments Act Title II
d. Rehabilitation Act Section 504

84. On which of the following do the Individuals with Disabilities Education Act and the Family Education Rights and Privacy Act differ with respect to student records?

a. Requiring instruction and training of educators on records confidentiality
b. Defining which student records are considered to be educational records
c. Determining conditions for destroying educational records via state laws
d. Regulating records collection, maintenance, confidentiality, or disclosure

85. What is the MOST accurate description among ways that effective school leaders openly share data with students and staff?

a. Involving identified students for developing data systems
b. Involving designated staff in developing assessment plans
c. Involving students in knowing and tracking their own data
d. Involving overall school data as the basis for student goals

86. How can school leaders best promote openness and collaborative decisions in ethical school leadership and make ethical conversation integral to their school culture?

a. They can analyze the ethical implications of any decision for the school community.
b. They can maintain constancy in their ethical frameworks throughout their careers.
c. They can accept needed funding even if the donors require less effective methods.
d. They can regularly initiate discussions for self-examination and ethics development.

87. The Council of Chief State School Officers (CCSSO) has set national Educational Leadership Policy Standards for school leaders to guide school communities in respecting individual worth and dignity. Which of the following is NOT specifically included among these standards?

a. Promoting staff professional growth
b. Students monitoring their own data
c. Assuring efficient school operations
d. Responding to community diversity

88. Research into school leader perceptions and attitudes regarding inclusive education of students with disabilities has found which of the following?

a. The majority of school leaders who were surveyed had positive attitudes toward inclusion.
b. School leaders who were exposed more to special education ideas had negative attitudes.
c. School leaders having positive experiences with disabilities made less restrictive placements.
d. Different categories of disability had no influence on school leaders' placement decisions.

89. Which of these can school leaders appropriately do to prevent or eliminate racism and ensure cultural equality in their schools?

a. They can change school board policies and also the school board's member composition.
b. They should train their faculty in mediation and conflict resolution skills to settle disputes.
c. They cannot do anything about minority student overrepresentation in special education.
d. They can make official policies not tolerating racism that suffice without consequences.

90. How can a school leader evaluate and improve the school curriculum for cultural and racial equity?

a. Instruct teachers to view curriculum as pluralistic and unchanging.
b. Include multicultural education within the school curriculum goals.
c. Assure books include diversity but not look for prejudiced content.
d. Focus multicultural education on foods, festivals, and fun activities.

91. Which statement is MOST accurate concerning how school leaders can ensure that faculty instructional practices treat minority students equitably?

a. Leaders can best get teachers to model appreciation of diversity for students by talking about it.

b. If teaching practices conflict with student cultures, leaders instruct teachers to be aware of this.

c. Having all teachers know a few words or phrases in each student's L1 is simply token lip service.

d. Leaders should make sure that all staff members learn to pronounce students' names correctly.

92. What has research by state education departments found about public perceptions of school leaders' roles?

a. The public believes school leaders most improve schools by requiring standardized tests for promotion.

b. The public believes school leaders most improve schools by recruiting and retaining superior teachers.

c. The public believes school leaders most improve schools by applying strategies to decrease class sizes.

d. The public believes school leaders most improve schools by getting more local control from the states.

93. Studies have found that student achievement is increased most by school investments in which of the following?

a. Expanding teacher education

b. Expanding teacher experience

c. Increasing the teacher salaries

d. Decreasing the sizes of classes

94. In isolating factors that affect student learning, researchers have found which of these has the most impact?

a. Family involvement and support

b. Family socioeconomic status

c. Qualifications of teachers

d. The sizes of classes

95. Researchers for state education departments report that school leaders they surveyed found which of the following to be their most important role?

a. Creating a supportive environment for teaching and learning

b. Supporting parent involvement in the education of students

c. Managing the school budget and procuring additional funds

d. Ensuring and maintaining safety and discipline in the school

96. What do experts recommend to school leaders for explaining policies to the school community?

a. Knowing and understanding policies are more important than communication skills.

b. Good communication skills take precedence over policy knowledge and understandings.

c. Making speeches to explain policies to parents is better than writing letters to them.

d. With safety policies and procedures, school leaders should conduct a formal review.

97. School leaders may be confronted by angry parents complaining about something that is outside of a leader's control. In the experiences of successful school leaders, which of the following is most effective?

a. Communicating that this is outside of their control
b. Listening and then communicating understanding
c. Responding to each parental complaint as it occurs
d. Referring the parent to somebody who has control

98. Which of the following MOST accurately represents expert recommendations for school leaders to promote educational equity by influencing curriculum interpretation?

a. Allowing harassed students to establish support networks
b. Communicating with staff periodically about equity beliefs
c. Clarifying misconceptions about equity, like deficit theories
d. Talking about diversity issues regardless of staff discomfort

99. Regarding school leader involvement in lobbying to influence legislation that affects education, which of these is true?

a. School leaders must inform lawmakers regarding educational issues.
b. School leaders cannot lobby for their schools on any individual basis.
c. School leaders can only lobby through a professional organization.
d. School leaders must be professional lobbyists to influence legislators.

100. Researchers have identified which of the following practices that successful education leaders recommend to advocate for educational excellence and equity?

a. They develop equity skills that spread through the learning community.
b. They study system inequities to discover solutions to the problems.
c. They study equitable leadership to discover their parts in the problems.
d. They advise others to develop collaborative approaches across systems.

Constructed Response

1. You are the principal of a school that historically was majority White, non-Hispanic/Latino, non-bilingual. Over the last ten years, the geographical area and your school in particular has experienced a profound change in its demographic makeup. This school year 75% of the student body is Hispanic/Latino, and 25% is White (non-Hispanic), with a large number of English Language Learners/Bilingual students. The staff of the school is predominately White, not bilingual, and has largely remained unchanged in ethnic makeup from previous year. A significant group of parents have become increasingly upset by what they perceive as a major communication barrier between parents, students, and school teachers/staff. The district Superintendent has asked you to develop a new cultural competency program aimed at solving this problem. In 300-600 words, outline the program you would come up with. Include how the program would be implemented and whom the program would include.

2. You are the principal of a large suburban high school with a diverse student and teacher population. One day you overhear a group of students discussing one of their classmates and her relationship with the chemistry teacher, Mr. Bolyn. The students are debating if their classmate and Mr. Bolyn have had sexual relations yet or not. In 150-300 words, explain how you would address this situation.

3. A group of parents have become increasingly disruptive at basketball games at the high school where you are the principal. There has been swearing, yelling, derogatory comments, etc., from the home bleachers. In 150-300 words, discuss how this situation could escalate, causing serious problems for the school, and outline the steps you would take to prevent this from happening.

4. You are starting your first year as principal at Mendoza High School, which has a diverse student population of about 1,500 students. Over the past several years the pass rate on the state mandated English exam has been declining and is now notably lower than the pass rate in other area high schools. Last school year (prior to your beginning at the school) the English department in conjunction with the faculty audited the school's curriculum and adjusted it to align with the state standards. This year, the superintendent has told you that you will have an additional $12,000 in discretionary funds to support the initiative to increase the pass rate of the English exam. In 300-600 words, outline two important issues you should consider when preparing recommendations for the discretionary budget, explain one strategy you can use to determine budget allocations to recommend that will promote improved student performance, and explain why the strategy you have described will likely be effective.

5. You are the principal of a 900-student middle school (6-8). The school recently formulated a school vision, which includes a critical goal of improving the academic and social-emotional preparedness of the school's eighth-graders for the transition to high school. Over the past several years, teachers and administrators in the local high school have become increasingly concerned about the level of preparedness of entering ninth-grade students. The ninth grades have been increasingly socially immature and lacking in vital academic and study skills. Various stakeholders (parents, students, teachers in both schools) attribute the problem to different reasons and would prescribe different remedies. You form a committee to formulate a plan to improve the readiness of the eighth graders in your school for their transition to high school. Committee members include teachers, parents, student supports (social worker, school psychologist), a special education representative, and a curriculum coordinator.

Write a 150-300 word memo to the members of the committee about the plan to improve eighth grade readiness for high school. Before you write the memo, state what assumptions you make about the school/community (rural/urban, demographics, socioeconomics). In the memo convey why you believe it is important for the school to succeed in this endeavor (improving preparedness for high school), describe 2-3 significant aspects of the school's instructional program that the committee will address in developing its plan. For each of these specific aspects/factors describe a type of data or other information that the team should analyze and explain why this type of information may be useful in analyzing the specific area of concern.

6. You are the principal of an 1800-student urban high school with a primarily African-American and Hispanic/Latino student population. The school has an active student newspaper with a much-beloved journalism teacher. Over the past several months, the student-staff have published several items of dubious origin that have caused controversy in the larger community. These items have typically had topics dealing with race relations. You have spoken to the journalism teacher after each incident about not allowing students to publish this type of questionable content. The newest issue of the student newspaper contains another such item. In 150-300 words, describe what you would do to address the situation.

7. You are the new principal of a 700-student elementary (K-5) school. The previous principal left the school in the midst of some controversy and there has been a significant turnover in teaching staff. In your first couple of weeks on the job, you notice a considerable amount of negativity among staff, in large part fomented by teachers who have been at the school for several years and have had multiple principals. In 300-600 words describe the strategies that you would use to address this negativity and change the culture of the school to a more positive tone and improve teacher and staff morale.

Answers and Explanations

1. C: The principal should help teachers design and deliver instruction that addresses the standards on which the test is based. Identifying individual students with the greatest needs (a) would help them but not writing instruction overall across all fourth-grade classes. Choices (b) and (d) reflect steps in the process of improving instruction, but neither should be the first step. Grouping student needs is most related to declining group test scores, so identifying those needs (c) is the first step to improve instruction.

2. A: Although meeting diverse student needs (b), implementing lesson plans accurately (c), and coordinating learning objectives with instructional materials and strategies (d) are all research-based best practices, only aligning lesson objectives with state grade-level English language arts (ELA) standards (a) directly addresses improving students' scores on state standardized ELA tests, which are based on those standards.

3. D: For making appropriate instructional decisions, the principal must be able to identify data required to inform them. Disaggregated standardized test data will inform identifying areas of student mastery and need, and state standards will inform designing curriculum and identifying instructional content. Knowing these together will inform identifying the best instructional strategies to increase student ELA achievement.

4. B: Although it is better for goals to be measurable, not all of them may be measurable for every student (a); it is more important that the principal identify which are measurable and which are not for every individual student (b). In particular, expectations must be measurable for all students (c) and aligned with the vision and goals. Whether a principal develops a vision, goals, and implementation plan alone or with staff varies, but research finds principal-staff collaboration more effective (d).

5. D: It is the school leader's responsibility to ensure that the individual school's vision, mission, and related goals are compatible with all policies issued not only at the building and school district level (a) and also at the level of the state education department (b) but also at the level of the federal (U.S.) education department (c).

6. C: Community business owners and employees are included among stakeholders in education; however, the school leader is less likely to survey them than those more key to this particular topic, including the superintendent of schools, administrators in the central office (a), members of the local school board, parents of the students (b), the students themselves, the teachers, and the paraprofessionals working at the school (d).

7. A: To gather this kind of feedback, the school leader should develop specific questions that are critical in nature and appropriate to this topic. Open-ended questions will stimulate discussions of many other stakeholder issues and concerns (b). Interviewing them all (c) is impracticable or at best very time inefficient. Discussion meetings (d) are both less focused like (b) and less time effective, like (c).

8. C: The school leader should share the commitment to implementing the school vision and goals not only with school personnel (a), (d), but also with community members (b), (c); these participants should not all share common perspectives (a), (b) but rather should represent the diversity of backgrounds and viewpoints in the school and community (c).

9. B: Researchers have found that the most effective school leaders have powerful influences over student achievement and school effectiveness; that these influences are indirect (a); that today's schools cannot be led by one principal without other educators' participating significantly (b); that the traditional model of single formal leadership neglects utilizing the valuable expertise of teachers (c); and that it is harder to sustain programs and improvements instituted under one principal after that principal leaves the school (d).

10. D: Researchers report a wide variety of school reform initiatives studied all commonly share one factor: leadership implicitly distributed among multiple individuals at schools. Studies also find that distributing leadership improves not only professional development of teachers (a) but also curriculum, assessment, and the development of professional communities in and among schools, led by teachers. Research finds the prodigious effort needed to make educational reform changes requires many good leaders, not just a few (b); broader-based capacity building requires distributing leadership more broadly, not limiting numbers of leaders (c).

11. C: Federal and state expectations of school principals typically include communicating not only the school vision and goals but also the school's continuing progress toward achieving the school goals to stakeholders (a); evaluating staff leadership abilities and developing and nurturing these (b); using consensus building and group process skills to support school reform efforts (c); and not only evaluating staff collaborative skills but also supporting staff needs in collaborative skills through professional development (d).

12. A: Progress toward different goals often is best assessed or monitored using different types of assessment instruments. For example, performance assessments or journals are more appropriate to assess analytical and critical thinking and communication skills than standardized achievement tests (b), which are more appropriate for monitoring progress in academic competence. Student progress in working more thoughtfully through cooperative learning skills would be more appropriately monitored through extended group projects (c) or teacher observations of students (d).

13. B: Successful school principals report that daily morning public announcements (a) are best for communicating school vision to students. For staff, a brief, succinct daily e-mail is best for combining and connecting administrative details and useful information with school vision (b), also showing that principals value staff time. Attending community events (c) is best for communicating school vision to stakeholders beyond campus. Effective meetings are two-way interactions (d), best for staff affirmation, collaborative opportunities, and internal highlight sharing. Most one-way communications can be handled through e-mails (b).

14. D: It would be most informative for the principal to ask a representative of the greatest variety of types of stakeholders to articulate the school vision to see if their responses are aligned or not. This will show how well he or she has communicated the vision to all involved rather than only comparing student and parent responses (a), only teacher and parent responses (b), or only different school staff members' responses (c).

15. B: Although most school faculties are too big to develop a vision statement as productively and/or effectively as smaller groups, the vision oversight team does not replace or represent faculty: It is imperative to have all faculty's full investment regardless (a). The team's primary purpose is to introduce the vision concept to faculty, engage them in writing a vision, facilitate the process, and synthesize their diverse input (b). The principal may select team members from the school leadership team (c) or other staff representing all school departments, offering leadership opportunities to those not formally educational leaders already (d).

16. A: Experts observe educators often assume "data" simply mean test results. They point out school vision oversight teams and faculty should also review other available data significant for informing school vision, including student attendance, absence, and tardiness data (b); rates of staff attendance, absence—including most frequent days—grade-level and department staff absenteeism, and turnover rates (c); student enrollments in extracurricular activities (clubs, sports, etc.); disciplinary incidents—including referral types, referring departments, teams, and teachers—and dispositions, including detention, in-school suspension, suspension, and expulsion (d).

17. C: Principals can help staff cope with changes by listening to and validating their thoughts through understanding common internal dialogues. These include wondering whether they will be able to live with and support the vision and also what is needed (a); whether they believe in their and the school's ability to realize it and also in the vision itself (b); whether they will be able to continue long-practiced traditions and why or why not (c); and what the vision will expect of them, how their life will change, and whether they will be able to maintain continuity in instructional practices (d).

18. B: To engage them in developing a vision statement, questions the vision oversight team can ask small groups of staff (eight or fewer) to discuss include the following: how their school differs from other schools (a); what they think their vision statement should reflect (b); what they need to do differently to realize the new vision (c); and what evidence they can identify that they are meeting the current vision (d). These topics elicit key values, beliefs, and ideas as the genesis of strong visions.

19. A: Researchers have documented practices of successful school principals relative to developing and sustaining clear school visions and learning goals, including protecting instructional time by scheduling building maintenance and limiting public announcements to minimize disruptions (a); expecting teachers and students to meet the goals they set (b); not only having a clear vision but, when needed, having two visions: one for their school and their own school role and another for their school's change process (c); and ensuring continual progress monitoring related directly to school goals (d).

20. D: Based on the research literature, experts draw these conclusions about school principals' roles in creating and realizing school visions and goals, including aligning instruction with them: Principals who focus on school improvement have more effective schools (a). Principals of high-achieving schools have equal confidence in themselves, their schools, and their teachers to meet school goals (b). To be effective, schools need principals who ensure instructional quality rather than delegating this role to others (c). Principals of high-achieving schools communicate to all stakeholders that the most important mission of the school is learning (d).

21. A: At one school that instituted a "no zeroes" grading policy, outcomes included that 72 percent fewer students received F grades; missed assignments decreased significantly (b); 57 percent fewer students received grades of D (c); and 68 percent fewer students received extra help (d) because they did not need it.

22. D: Research found black and Latino students completed less homework, even though they spent similar amounts of time (a) as white and Asian students. Researchers attributed differences in grades and homework not to student motivation or effort (b) but to gaps in student skills and differences in home supports (d). Asian students had higher grades and finished more homework by spending more time (c) on studying and homework.

23. B: Student trust in the teacher and interest in the class lead to success versus mistrust and disinterest (a). Ambition in learning leads to success versus ambivalence toward learning (c). Industry in pursuing learning goals promotes student success versus disengagement from boredom or discouragement from difficulty (d). However, success is more likely through a balance of student autonomy and teacher control versus too much of either one (b).

24. A: Effective professional development (PD) is student centered, not teacher centered, and requires active teacher involvement in the learning process. Job-embedded, school-based PD can be outside the school if it emerges from and contributes to classroom practices and teachers perceive it as part of their daily work; it requires teachers to collaboratively problem solve (b). PD must be supported and ongoing; teachers must know and understand both underlying theories and their practical applications (c). PD must be part of district-supported, systematic reform, but school leaders should not let it cover new trends or fads that are unstudied, hence unsupported (d).

25. C: For developing professional learning communities (PLCs) and identifying effective instructional practices, experts recommend school leaders form staff teams whose members collaborate in accomplishing commonly shared, not diverse, goals (a); assign teams to develop and administer formative assessments and design curriculum (b); work with teams to identify both exemplary and struggling teachers and students (c); and participate with teams to develop coordinated intervention plans for struggling students (d).

26. D: Community outreach, encouraging family volunteers, and serving on PTAs is predominantly the responsibility of school leaders, rather than the collective responsibility of school leaders. Supporting parenting skills (a), actively participating in and encouraging parents to participate in student learning, and engaging parents to become partners for school decision making are collaborative efforts, as the teachers, faculty, and staff are likely to have much more direct contact with the parents than a school leader is capable of maintaining. These processes help to build a school community and are supported throughout the community, not only by the leadership.

27. A: When a school leader attends a district school board meeting in an unfamiliar community, he is likely to encounter issues that were not prevalent in his previous community. If he is receptive to change, he is likely to expand his understanding of issues and grow as a school leader by experiencing a variety of perspectives. Seeing areas of disagreement (b) and seeing differences between district and school vision(d) can be helpful in addressing conflict and working to unify a school or district's vision, but is does not necessarily help develop the school leader's perspectives. Learning to run school board meetings (c) does not help with developing beliefs about educational issues.

28. D: The collective work of all leaders adds up to more than the sum of its parts (a) in the holistic form of distributed leadership, which emphasizes interdependent leadership (d). One way of describing interdependence is that all members realize they must "sink or swim" together, not individually (c). The additive form of distributive leadership, everybody is a leader, regardless of whether or how the members interact. In the additive form, the leadership members are responsible for solitary parts and do not have to coordinate regarding their domains. In the additive model, leadership members work relatively independently on their goals, while in the holistic model, leadership works closely together and coordinate on many shared goals and tasks. With this in mind, (a) and (c) are wrong because they refer to the wrong form. Answer (b) is wrong in that in the holistic form, leaders are distinct, but work together.

29. B: Ways that school leaders have appropriately involved students in school improvement efforts include allowing students to plan school-wide forums (a), conduct school-wide surveys (b),

participate in hiring school leaders (c), and testify before education committees in their state legislatures, which is not illegal (d).

30. B: To create environments wherein teachers feel safe to express their ideas, school leaders should not criticize even unusual ideas (a); schedule regular, brief times during meetings for teachers to express original ideas (b); abandon their fears that teachers will undermine their authority (c) because leadership experts find that the more a leader shares power, the more authority he or she gains; and ask teachers what elements of a safe environment are similar, not different, for teachers in the school as for students in their classrooms (d).

31. C: Educational researchers have found that principals taking traditional authoritarian roles are not respected by teachers (a); teachers resent authoritarian principals' control as manipulative, leading to teacher job dissatisfaction, but appreciate more freedom in curriculum design (b) and other work areas; and teachers attribute their classroom success to empowerment by principals who give them freedom to take appropriate risks (c), which school leaders must encourage to meet student needs (d).

32. D: Teachers are more receptive to principal feedback that is not unexpected (a): principals should tell teachers their expectations and encourage teachers to establish goals before offering feedback related to these (b). As behaviorism has shown, effective feedback is immediate, not delayed (c). Effective feedback strategies include identifying teacher strengths first and then communicating criticisms in the form of requesting solutions (d).

33. A: Calibration is the process of exploring and reaching consensus about learning standards, goals, and definitions at building, system-wide, and district-wide levels. Student data focus (b) yields in-depth information, for example, how well students are meeting specific, time-limited learning objectives. Student profiles assist cross-curricular teams. Summative assessment data aid capacity building, help identify pedagogical strengths and needs and specific remedial student groups, and politically support long-term strategic information plans. Educator engagement (c) alleviates faculty mistrust under external accountability pressures and facilitates systemic, sustainable change. Supportive technology (d) facilitates teacher access to data and shares reciprocal support with data team collaboration.

34. B: Realizing the value of good PD, promoting teacher participation, and communicating PD benefits to key stakeholders (b) are characteristics of strong school leaders. Valuing ongoing learning and promoting continuous improvement, inquiry, collaboration, and problem solving (a) are characteristics of vibrant learning communities as professional development (PD) contexts. Human, financial, and temporal contributions, and assessments of allocation coordination and investment returns (c), are characteristics of sufficient resources and their effective use. Analyzing student data to identify proficiency standards, learning gaps, and assessment and behavioral results (d) is characteristic of rigorous data analysis by schools and districts.

35. D: Incorporating new and different instructional goals (d) does not necessarily help with providing rigorous and relevant curriculum design. Significant purposes of rigorous, relevant curriculum design include challenging educator thinking about ways students learn (a) and how they evaluate these; incorporating teachers' instructional skills (b); and applying a structure to organize existing instruction and assessment goals (c) but not introducing new and/or different instructional goals.

36. A: The philosophy of differentiating instruction is compatible with standards-based instruction required for accountability as long as educators apply principles of effective curriculum and

instruction. For example, differentiation principles include these: leading students into Vygotsky's Zone of Proximal Development (where students can do more with assistance than they can alone) optimizes learning (a). So do natural learning opportunities (b). Activating prior student knowledge not only makes new learning relevant to students but also enables them to learn best (c). Sense of community, wherein students feel respected and important, makes learning more effective both socially and academically (d).

37. C: Effective teachers combine standards-based instruction, enabling students to pass accountability exams with differentiated instruction and addressing individual student differences in skills and learning levels, using teaching methods including these: starting every textbook chapter by defining specific skills and concepts for students to master in each curriculum segment (a); allotting comparable small-group times for advanced, struggling, and mixed-level students (b); dividing classroom time among whole-class, small-group, teacher-led, and independent activities (c); and guiding students to connect new material to their prior learning (d).

38. A: School leaders are responsible for deciding how often and to whom teachers submit data; for example, they might want teachers to submit data every 2 to 3 weeks to their team leaders to enable structured data discussions during team meetings. School leaders are responsible to ensure teachers collect data continuously: quarterly (b) is insufficient to adjust instruction, can impede viewing monitoring as essential, and fails to further faculty instruction and assessment goals. School leaders are also responsible for helping faculty choose and develop data-recording forms (c) and ensuring faculty application of state-assigned rubrics to predict student performance on state assessments (d).

39. D: School leaders must collaborate with faculty and other staff to design curriculum and instruction (a); review programs regularly not only to determine correct implementation (b) but also to identify students' unmet educational needs despite implementing programs accurately (c); and in the event of such unmet needs, help faculty and other staff identify content and practices that will address these (d).

40. B: The practice recommended by education authorities is for principals to collaborate with not only curriculum specialists and school professionals (a), for example, faculty, educational specialists, therapists, and so on; not only students and professionals (c); and not only professionals and board of education members (d) but curriculum specialists, professionals, and members of the board of education in making curriculum decisions.

41. D: School leaders must know how to help teachers learn new instructional methods, and how to predict how long it will take for them to learn these (a); how much time effective planning takes, which varies with the number of students to be taught (b); how to network teachers learning new approaches as the school leaders implement these approaches (c); and how much time effective planning will take, which also varies with the levels at which teachers will instruct students in academic content (d).

42. C: Teaching the same content across all classrooms at the same grade levels (a), and teaching content aligned with state and/or district assessments and standards (b) are characteristics of horizontal curriculum alignment. Teaching content that progresses through grade levels, incorporating scaffolding to prepare students for the next grade (d), is characteristic of vertical alignment. Teaching to minimize achievement gaps through standardizing education (c) is accomplished through both horizontal and vertical curriculum alignment.

43. A: School leaders should use their analyses of these elements of teacher curriculum, instruction, and assessment implementation to determine how well they align with one another, within (c) and across (d) grade levels, across the curriculum (a), and with state and/or national standards (b) as well.

44. C: School leaders should lead teachers to encourage solid student comprehension of concepts first, and only encourage students to use technology for enhancing their research and problem-solving skills after, not before (a), they understand concepts. They should not only lead but require teachers to instruct students in legal and ethical issues with accessing and using technology (b) and clearly differentiate with teachers between learning targets for student technology skills and learning targets for student thinking and content quality (d).

45. A: School leaders who form data inquiry teams of teachers should direct these teams to develop action plans based on their analyses of student assessment data. They should assign the teams to implement these plans; supporting their implementation (b) is the school leader's job. School leaders should direct teams to analyze data from both formative and summative assessments (c) by classes, student subgroups, and individual students (d).

46. A: Research conducted over recent decades finds that although socioeconomic status (SES) correlates strongly with student academic achievement, both available school resources and school curriculum correlate even more strongly with student achievement than SES. Researchers say these findings should motivate school leaders and schools to reduce achievement gaps rather than blame them on family or community SES.

47. D: Experts recommend that school leaders not simply complete a checklist for classroom visits (a) but further student success through improving teacher instructional quality by applying their observations of classroom instructional practices. School leaders should give both individual teachers feedback, through conversations and written communications, and collective teacher feedback (b), through providing statistics (d). They can produce formative feedback through making walk-throughs (c) and both formative and summative feedback through making formal observations.

48. A: Expert recommendations for school leaders in the best use of school-wide student achievement data include instituting supports for developing a data-driven school culture (a); instructing students to understand and use their own data (b) to set learning goals; developing and maintaining data systems on a district-wide basis (c); and incorporating data as an essential component of a cycle of continuous instructional improvement (d).

49. C: School-wide data teams should not hold school staff accountable for using data (a), supervise staff data activities (b), or assume the role of giving expert advice to school staff (d) about using data. Rather they should lead the school staff by example through modeling the effective use of data (c) for improving instruction and meeting school goals.

50. D: To collaborate effectively with teachers regarding assessment, school leaders must know classroom assessment principles, including that no assessment instrument is error free (a)—that is, all assessment involves some error; that authors and users of assessments typically underestimate testing error (b); that reliability, that is, getting consistent results across repeated administrations, applies to test scores and not the tests themselves (c); and that good assessment is not only valid (tests what it means or claims to test) and reliable but also ethical and fair (d).

51. B: In recent decades, environmental quality issues have emerged that affect school facility operations management. These include asbestos, radon, and other hazardous materials control;

energy conservation; and improvement of water, indoor air quality, and acoustics, which may involve district support in hiring expert facility consultants. School leaders have government guidelines for food services (a); transportation (c) and custodial (d) services have existed longer than environmental awareness, have school policies and procedures in place, and are less likely to require expert consultation.

52. B: School leaders are directly responsible for allocating budget for school maintenance and inspections. They should assign experienced maintenance supervisors to develop specific inspection and maintenance procedures (a) and schedules (c) and should oversee the implementation of preventive maintenance procedures, which they cannot directly implement by themselves (d).

53. C: Among school principals' roles in leading the implementation of school-wide technology adoption, prioritizing change and supporting and encouraging faculty (a) are responsibilities associated with the role of motivator and cheerleader. Assuring teachers have what they need to meet change goals (b) is associated with the role of resource provider. Establishing conditions for change by setting standards for learning and collaboration (c) is associated with the role of learning organization leader. Leading change initiatives, resolving problems, and providing learning opportunities for faculty (d) are associated with the role of facilitator.

54. A: The National Education Association (NEA) identifies essential components of any school Acceptable Use Policy (AUP), including a preamble and definition section; an acceptable uses section (b), defining appropriate student internet use; an unacceptable uses section (c), defining prohibited uses, behaviors, and Web sites; a policy statement (d) identifying covered services and student use conditions; and a violation and sanctions section (a) informing students how to question policy applications and report violations, which may conform to the general school disciplinary code.

55. D: School district personnel and school leaders can predict employee salaries more easily than benefits (a), particularly health-care benefits, which have been changing recently due to both new federal legislation and health-care provider practices. Estimating the next school year's budget expenses must include reserving funds for unexpected emergencies (b) like unplanned facility repairs. Districts issue school budgets for school leaders that display revenue allocation figures side by side with enrollment figures (c) for easier reference. Transportation expenses can be among the most necessary and costly yet are not reflected in school budgets (d).

56. D: Researchers have found that more effective schools can fill vacancies by recruiting and hiring more effective teachers from other schools (a); they assign new teachers among students using more equitable methods (b); teachers improve faster after hiring in more effective schools than in less effective schools (c); and more effective schools have greater ability to retain higher-quality teachers than less effective schools do (d).

57. B: These are activities that school leaders can ask staff to participate in to increase their skill and knowledge bases. The (a) activities are ways school leaders can get staff involved in school leadership to develop these skills. The (c) activities are ways school leaders can offer staff opportunities for observation and reflection to develop leadership skills. The (d) activities are ways school leaders can support staff participation in professional development to promote leadership skills.

58. A: Goals for school leaders related to their school safety plans include leading school needs assessments, safety plan development, and implementation monitoring; developing a system to

track, report, and give feedback on school incidents and crime and communicating this information to stakeholders (b); designing safe traffic patterns to, from, and within the school rather than appointing others to do this (c); and not only adopting emergency evacuation procedures but also adopting crisis management procedures for the school rather than delegating this (d).

59. C: Developing a school safety plan requires participation by the entire community because schools with the most numerous and severe violence and crime incidents are in communities with the same characteristics. School leaders and staff are not the only ones (a) because addressing community issues reflected in schools requires collaboration among resources contributing varied expertise and because schools are for learning, not controlling (b) violence or crime. Not only law enforcement and mental health personnel (d) but also parents, community leaders, business leaders, and other community professionals serving youth should participate as well as students, teachers, and administrators.

60. A: That No Child Left Behind's stress on accountability has shifted school counselors' responsibilities away from mental health (MH) toward academic performance, reducing professional support services, represents limited resources. That students are routinely diagnosed with serious disorders and prescribed costly treatments, despite the fact that prevention and MH promotion can address most issues (b), represents inadequate research. That MH resources are not proportionate or equitable (c) represents uneven resource distribution. That cultural traditions marginalize school MH priority (d) represents stigmatizing MH issues.

61. D: External stressors (a) can exist in the home, community, and/or school. Educational problems (b) can originate within the individual student (e.g., learning disabilities [LD] and attention deficit hyperactivity disorder [ADHD]), family, community, and/or school. Psychosocial problems (c) can often be prevented or addressed in schools. However, psychological disorders (d) are LEAST likely to be caused or treated in schools, typically requiring psychotherapeutic treatment and often therapy plus medication.

62. C: Whereas the National Association of Secondary School Principals (NASSP) recommends staff training in all these areas, strategies promoting school-wide positive environments are most related to Response to Intervention (RtI). RtI involves instituting school-wide positive learning and behavioral supports with three tiers of progressively more intensive intervention. Whereas the first tier includes universal screening, which relates to early identification (a), all three tiers benefit from school-wide positive supports, including students in Tiers 2 and 3, who receive additional interventions. Referrals (b) are only made for students not responding in Tier 3 and/or responding but needing additional services. Cooperative school models (d) are beneficial irrespective of using or not using RtI.

63. A: Conducting drills prepares school staff for responding in a timely, organized, efficient manner in the event of an actual emergency. Drills do not prevent (b) emergencies but prepare people for them. Though response (c) is prominently featured in the question description as the focus of drills, staff are not actually responding during drills but preparing to respond if or when the need should arise. Recovery (d) follows response; neither occurs without an actual emergency.

64. D: The Incident Command System (ICS) planning (a) function collects and evaluates data, identifies issues, develops action plans, and recommends future actions. The logistics (b) function identifies services and resources needed to support incident response needs. The command (c) function is responsible for overall incident management, public safety, information, and community agency liaisons. The operations (d) function develops objectives, organizes resources, and directs resources and actions to incident response. (The other ICS function is finance.)

65. B: School leaders must not only communicate feedback from monitoring safety plan implementation to school staff and students; they must also document this feedback (a). They must document their observations from monitoring safety plan implementation (b). They must document not only school incidents disrupting safety but also related feedback they give to stakeholders (c). School leaders are responsible for documenting safety management procedures they adopt, but they may designate others to document these (d).

66. B: In many American states and communities, schools are the only, or main, mental health (MH) service providers for children (a). Because services like clinical psychiatric care are unfeasible and inappropriate in schools (b), school and community MH services must be integrated within the care continuum. Students and parents are more comfortable getting MH help with familiar school settings and staff (c). Research studies show students are more likely to seek counseling services in schools (d).

67. C: Researchers have found segregated services more likely to cause isolated skill development and fragmentation, whereas integrated comprehensive services require cross-disciplinary sharing of specific educator expertise, benefiting students (a) and colleagues alike. Although its staff design must be student based, a principle underlying integrated comprehensive services is that the source of student failure is the system, not the student (b). School leaders and other educators integrating services should design curriculum and instruction beginning with differentiation (c) rather than adapt it afterward (d).

68. B: School leaders and other educators should involve families in collaborative educational design as they are their children's primary advocates (a). Families can advocate for other families within school-based dialogues (c), and they can offer service and support to schools in developing learning communities (d). However, when family participation is limited to an elite minority who volunteer, other families are more likely to feel intimidated against participating than inspired to participate (b).

69. C: Some successful school leaders find sharing real estate data with the business community shows how better schools raise property values and local consumer spending (a). More local families attend schools when leaders share improved student test scores with them (b). Whereas significantly improved test scores for students in minority groups that typically experience achievement gaps are best shared within the first year (c) to encourage and attract minority families, school leaders find it better to share overall school academic gains over several years, when these gains are more substantial (d).

70. A: Community partners can establish relationships that afford students greater social capital, which empowers their successful interactions beyond the community. Community partners also can expedite student and family access to services (b), which meet their physical, mental, and social needs more than contributing to global competency; give students safe contexts for experimentation and leadership (c); and offer adult guidance and positive role models (d), contributing to physical, intellectual, emotional, and social development and academic and nonacademic skills overall more than to specific, real-world, interactional success.

71. D: Researchers find that public engagement in education strengthens local safety and security (a), improves public perceptions of school reform efforts (b), revitalizes communities as well as helping schools (c), and increases the participation of citizens and students in both school service and community service (d).

72. B: Using a constructivist model to incorporate multiple stakeholder perspectives, school leaders first identify who stakeholders are then discover their concerns; supply a method and frame of reference for obtaining and analyzing stakeholders' input; and bring stakeholder groups to consensus. If consensus building hits an impasse, leaders should have an agenda for negotiations; procure and disseminate information for negotiating with disagreeing stakeholders; and establish a forum for negotiations. Once negotiations are concluded, school leaders make and deliver a report to the stakeholders and then review any unresolved stakeholder issues.

73. A: Measures of how school community engagement strategies affect students include their greater academic achievement and fewer school behavior problems (a); increased school attendance and increased school enrollment (b); higher school enrollment and achievement (c); and increased satisfaction along with achievement (d).

74. C: School leaders who have engaged communities and families in school reform initiatives have found that their efforts resulted in more parent attendance not only to school events and meetings but also to school seminars, workshops, and other trainings (a). School leaders' outreach to families also resulted in more family-to-school outreach (b). More parents became advocates and organizers for school improvement (c). And both community members and parents responded by serving on school or advisory councils (d), actively participating in creating school policies, programs, and practices.

75. B: Improving the resources and methods available for collecting data is one way that state education departments can support school leaders in their jobs by facilitating their analyses of school strengths, needs, progress, trends, and so on. Another way state education departments can support school leaders in their jobs is by creating more learning opportunities for them (a), (c), (d).

76. D: Having multilingual staff interpret (a) addresses language differences. Suggesting parents ask children about assignments instead of helping with homework (b) addresses limited parental literacy and/or education by helping parents support children in nonliterate ways. Designating parent or community rooms where parents and other community members can meet with other parents and teachers and access information (c) addresses needs for linguistically, culturally, economically, and educationally diverse stakeholders; those with hectic schedules; and everybody else. Hiring community liaisons to help staff understand diverse parental beliefs about education (d), for example, that educators are authority figures they should never question, addresses cultural differences.

77. C: School-community interagency collaborations enable participants to develop shared visions and missions for education and service (a); pool their resources and funds for common purposes (b); offer multiple services, all within the same school setting (c); and exchange student and family information: although privacy laws like HIPAA, FERPA, parts of IDEA, and so on keep health-care or education agencies from disclosing health or education records, parents can give written informed consent; regardless, collaborators can still exchange much information about students and families without involving official records (d).

78. A: Effective school leaders must clarify what they need, what stakeholders want, and how these can coincide to communicate and determine partnership feasibility. They must adjust language for businesspeople. For example, business executives use more proactive than reactive language (b). School leaders should determine whether their visions and/or missions match other's, but these need not match exactly (c): they can overlap—and school leaders must identify these overlaps. Though a few rare businesspeople are altruistically motivated by school benefits, most must hear what they will get from partnership (d).

79. B: Through experience, school leaders have found that simply asking prospective community partners to listen to what they have to say (a) can often communicate their school's needs. Some have found sharing the story of their school communicated what their schools needed (c). Clearly identifying their school's assets and greatest needs (d) helps school leaders and community partners both define their expectations. Asking community leaders how their own experiences with education influenced who they are now (b) motivates their engagement and assistance by enabling meaningful connections between personal experience and school partnership.

80. A: "Build out" refers to building upon successful initiatives by sharing the results and supporting extended endeavors. "Spell out" (b) refers to defining the purposes and terms of a partnership, including each individual's duties and deadlines. "Work out" (c) refers to addressing problems as they occur and modifying approaches as needed. "Reach out" (d) refers to offering prospective community partners by offering them specific help in their own territories.

81. C: Obeying federal, state, and local laws and regulations (II) and implementing the local board of education's administrative regulations and policies (V) could both conflict with acting to change laws and regulations that are against valid education goals (IV), or vice versa, as obeying and implementing laws, regulations, and policies can be countermanded by acting to change laws, regulations, or policies.

82. D: Choices (a), (b), and (c) are almost identical word for word between the American Association of School Administrators (AASA) Code of Ethics for Educational Leaders and the National Association of Secondary School Principals (NASSP) recommendations for a code of ethical conduct, as are most of their other items. However, the AASA Code of Ethics additionally includes two statements of standards for school leaders to accept responsibility and accountability for their own actions and to commit to serving others above self (d). These are not included in the NASSP recommendations.

83. B: The Civil Rights Act of 1964 (a) protects everyone, including students, against discrimination for multiple reasons. The Americans with Disabilities Act (ADA, 1973) protects individuals against discrimination for disabilities; Title II of the ADA Amendments Act of 2008 (c) protects students with disabilities from discrimination by requiring equal opportunities to benefit from government programs, services, and activities, including education. Section 504 of the Rehabilitation Act of 1973, amended 2003 (d), also protects students with disabilities against discrimination. The 1974 Family Educational Rights and Privacy Act (FERPA) protects student education records privacy; the Individuals with Disabilities Act (IDEA) does this for students with disabilities (b).

84. A: The Individuals with Disabilities Education Act (IDEA) and Family Rights and Privacy Act (FERPA) both define the same document types as educational records (b). FERPA determines conditions for educational records destruction based on state laws (c). IDEA amendments regarding educational records collection, maintenance, confidentiality, disclosure (d), and destruction (c) are based on FERPA. However, the IDEA requires designating special education records custodians to ensure the instruction and training of all educators collecting confidential information, but FERPA does not (a).

85. C: Effective school leaders involve all students in developing systems for collecting, analyzing, applying, incorporating, and sharing data rather than only identifying some students to involve (a); involve all staff members in participating in developing assessment plans rather than designating certain members (b); involve students closely in knowing and monitoring their own data (c); and basing individual student goals on each student's specific data measures, not just on overall school data (d).

86. D: School leaders should not analyze only ethical implications of decisions for the school community (a) but habituate every member to such analysis to guide their approaches. Because total experience and learning contribute to their development, ethical frameworks should grow throughout school leaders' careers, not remain constant (b). Ethical school leaders never accept funding from donors requiring less effective methods (c). By regularly engaging staff and stakeholders in conversations helping them self-examine assumptions and develop ethical understanding (d), school leaders integrate ethical discussion into school culture.

87. B: The Council of Chief State School Officers (CCSSO) standards include developing school cultures and instructional programs promoting student learning and staff professional growth (a); assuring safe, effective learning environments through efficient management of school resources, organization, and operations (c); and responding to needs and interests of diverse community members (d), among others. However, they do not include having students monitor their own data (b), which is otherwise an exemplary school leader policy but not part of these standards for respecting individual worth and dignity.

88. C: Research from the Council for Exceptional Children has found that of elementary school leaders surveyed, only 20 percent had positive attitudes toward inclusion (a) of students with disabilities. That minority of school leaders with such positive attitudes had more exposure to special education concepts (b) and more positive experiences with students having disabilities, making them more likely to place them into less restrictive settings (c). School leaders also had different experiences and made different placements depending on different student disability categories (d).

89. A: School leaders can change not only school board policies if they find these lacking racial or cultural sensitivity but also board composition to represent the student population. They should train students in mediation and conflict resolutions skills for settling disputes (b). When minority students are overrepresented in special education, they can do something by administering culturally fair tests and revisiting eligibility determinations based on results (c). They should not only make official policies against tolerating racism but also clearly define consequences (d) for racist behaviors.

90. B: To evaluate curriculum for cultural and racial equity and improve it as needed, school leaders can instruct teachers to view curriculum as pluralistic and constantly changing to meet changing student populations and needs (a); include multicultural education in the school's curriculum goals (b); not only make sure books contain diversity but also have teachers examine books for prejudiced or discriminatory content (c); and include multicultural education in books, other media, and learning experiences rather than focus it on only foods, festivals, and fun activities (d).

91. D: The best way to get teachers to model for students is for school leaders to model for teachers rather than only talking about it (a). If teaching practices conflict with student cultural beliefs, values, or practices, leaders must instruct teachers to replace or change these, not simply be aware of the conflict (b). Having all teachers know a few words or phrases in each student's first language (L1) makes classrooms welcoming, psychologically safe learning environments (c). Similarly, leaders should ensure all staff members learn to pronounce students' names correctly (d).

92. B: Research by state education departments finds the public believes school leaders improve schools by recruiting and retaining better teachers more than by requiring standardized tests for grade promotion (a), applying strategies to decrease class sizes (c), or getting state education departments to give local schools more control (d). This shows public perceptions of the importance of the school leader's role in teacher qualification and professional development.

93. A: Studies comparing school investments have found that investing in expanding teacher education (a) increases student achievement more than expanding teacher experience (b), increasing teacher salaries (c), or decreasing class size (d). This is significant considering how many critics have blamed lack of student achievement on new or inexperienced teachers, inadequate teacher payment, and excessive class sizes more than on lack of teacher professional development.

94. C: Researchers have found that among family involvement and support (a), family socioeconomic status (b), qualifications of teachers (c), and the sizes of classes (d), 44 percent of the impact on student learning is attributed to teacher qualifications. This means that the other 56 percent of the impact is divided among the other three factors; so of these four factors, teacher qualifications have the most impact on student learning.

95. A: School leaders surveyed by state education department researchers believed that creating a supportive environment for teaching and learning was their most important role, superseding their roles of supporting parental involvement in education (b), managing school budgets and obtaining more funds (c), or maintaining school safety and discipline (d).

96. D: School leaders must combine enough knowledge and understanding of policies to follow and administer them (a) with good enough communication skills to explain them to the school community (b). Regarding school safety policies and procedures in particular, experts from the National Association of School Psychologists (NASP) recommend school leaders write letters to parents for their reference. Parents cannot remember or review this information from speeches (c). NASP also recommends school leaders conduct formal reviews of safety policies and procedures (d) to assure they address all potential issues.

97. B: Telling already agitated parents that their complaint is outside the school leader's control (a) will only exacerbate their frustration, as will putting them off by referring them to someone else (d). Answering each parental complaint as it occurs (c) interrupts the parent, who will perceive this as defensiveness and/or disinterest in getting to the root of the problem. Experienced school leaders report many parents simply want them to listen to everything they say; others add that communicating understanding (b), which shows compassion and concern, is critical.

98. C: Experts recommend that school leaders establish support networks for harassed students as part of creating safe, welcoming school environments that make all students feel valued. School leaders have far more knowledge and means for creating such networks than students (a). Rather than talk with staff periodically, experts say school leaders should model equity beliefs for them through daily interactions (b). They should also clarify misconceptions related to equity, like deficit theories (c), and encourage staff to be comfortable discussing diversity issues (d), values, and social justice.

99. A: From their direct involvement with schools and school districts, school leaders are most knowledgeable about educational issues; therefore, lawmakers need to hear from them about these issues to inform the bill they get passed. School leaders can lobby for their schools as individuals (b), or through community contacts (e.g., local businesses, community leaders, and local politicians), or through their professional organizations (c). The largest professional organizations for school administrators have their own registered lobbying staffs. School leaders need not be professional lobbyists (d) to influence legislators.

100. D: Researchers report that to advocate for excellence and equity in education, successful education leaders follow and recommend giving staff, colleagues, and other learning community members opportunities to develop equity skills. Developing their own equity skills will not

automatically spread these through the learning community (a). Successful school leaders study system inequities to discover how they are part of the problems (b) and study equitable leadership characteristics to discover solutions to the problems (c). Additionally, they advise others to develop collaborative approaches across systems (d), enabling exploration of varying perspectives on leadership practices.

How to Overcome Test Anxiety

Just the thought of taking a test is enough to make most people a little nervous. A test is an important event that can have a long-term impact on your future, so it's important to take it seriously and it's natural to feel anxious about performing well. But just because anxiety is normal, that doesn't mean that it's helpful in test taking, or that you should simply accept it as part of your life. Anxiety can have a variety of effects. These effects can be mild, like making you feel slightly nervous, or severe, like blocking your ability to focus or remember even a simple detail.

If you experience test anxiety—whether severe or mild—it's important to know how to beat it. To discover this, first you need to understand what causes test anxiety.

Causes of Test Anxiety

While we often think of anxiety as an uncontrollable emotional state, it can actually be caused by simple, practical things. One of the most common causes of test anxiety is that a person does not feel adequately prepared for their test. This feeling can be the result of many different issues such as poor study habits or lack of organization, but the most common culprit is time management. Starting to study too late, failing to organize your study time to cover all of the material, or being distracted while you study will mean that you're not well prepared for the test. This may lead to cramming the night before, which will cause you to be physically and mentally exhausted for the test. Poor time management also contributes to feelings of stress, fear, and hopelessness as you realize you are not well prepared but don't know what to do about it.

Other times, test anxiety is not related to your preparation for the test but comes from unresolved fear. This may be a past failure on a test, or poor performance on tests in general. It may come from comparing yourself to others who seem to be performing better or from the stress of living up to expectations. Anxiety may be driven by fears of the future—how failure on this test would affect your educational and career goals. These fears are often completely irrational, but they can still negatively impact your test performance.

Review Video: 3 Reasons You Have Test Anxiety
Visit mometrix.com/academy and enter code: 428468

Elements of Test Anxiety

As mentioned earlier, test anxiety is considered to be an emotional state, but it has physical and mental components as well. Sometimes you may not even realize that you are suffering from test anxiety until you notice the physical symptoms. These can include trembling hands, rapid heartbeat, sweating, nausea, and tense muscles. Extreme anxiety may lead to fainting or vomiting. Obviously, any of these symptoms can have a negative impact on testing. It is important to recognize them as soon as they begin to occur so that you can address the problem before it damages your performance.

Review Video: 3 Ways to Tell You Have Test Anxiety
Visit mometrix.com/academy and enter code: 927847

The mental components of test anxiety include trouble focusing and inability to remember learned information. During a test, your mind is on high alert, which can help you recall information and stay focused for an extended period of time. However, anxiety interferes with your mind's natural processes, causing you to blank out, even on the questions you know well. The strain of testing during anxiety makes it difficult to stay focused, especially on a test that may take several hours. Extreme anxiety can take a huge mental toll, making it difficult not only to recall test information but even to understand the test questions or pull your thoughts together.

Review Video: How Test Anxiety Affects Memory
Visit mometrix.com/academy and enter code: 609003

Effects of Test Anxiety

Test anxiety is like a disease—if left untreated, it will get progressively worse. Anxiety leads to poor performance, and this reinforces the feelings of fear and failure, which in turn lead to poor performances on subsequent tests. It can grow from a mild nervousness to a crippling condition. If allowed to progress, test anxiety can have a big impact on your schooling, and consequently on your future.

Test anxiety can spread to other parts of your life. Anxiety on tests can become anxiety in any stressful situation, and blanking on a test can turn into panicking in a job situation. But fortunately, you don't have to let anxiety rule your testing and determine your grades. There are a number of relatively simple steps you can take to move past anxiety and function normally on a test and in the rest of life.

Review Video: How Test Anxiety Impacts Your Grades
Visit mometrix.com/academy and enter code: 939819

Physical Steps for Beating Test Anxiety

While test anxiety is a serious problem, the good news is that it can be overcome. It doesn't have to control your ability to think and remember information. While it may take time, you can begin taking steps today to beat anxiety.

Just as your first hint that you may be struggling with anxiety comes from the physical symptoms, the first step to treating it is also physical. Rest is crucial for having a clear, strong mind. If you are tired, it is much easier to give in to anxiety. But if you establish good sleep habits, your body and mind will be ready to perform optimally, without the strain of exhaustion. Additionally, sleeping well helps you to retain information better, so you're more likely to recall the answers when you see the test questions.

Getting good sleep means more than going to bed on time. It's important to allow your brain time to relax. Take study breaks from time to time so it doesn't get overworked, and don't study right before bed. Take time to rest your mind before trying to rest your body, or you may find it difficult to fall asleep.

Review Video: The Importance of Sleep for Your Brain
Visit mometrix.com/academy and enter code: 319338

Along with sleep, other aspects of physical health are important in preparing for a test. Good nutrition is vital for good brain function. Sugary foods and drinks may give a burst of energy but this burst is followed by a crash, both physically and emotionally. Instead, fuel your body with protein and vitamin-rich foods.

Also, drink plenty of water. Dehydration can lead to headaches and exhaustion, especially if your brain is already under stress from the rigors of the test. Particularly if your test is a long one, drink water during the breaks. And if possible, take an energy-boosting snack to eat between sections.

Review Video: How Diet Can Affect your Mood
Visit mometrix.com/academy and enter code: 624317

Along with sleep and diet, a third important part of physical health is exercise. Maintaining a steady workout schedule is helpful, but even taking 5-minute study breaks to walk can help get your blood pumping faster and clear your head. Exercise also releases endorphins, which contribute to a positive feeling and can help combat test anxiety.

When you nurture your physical health, you are also contributing to your mental health. If your body is healthy, your mind is much more likely to be healthy as well. So take time to rest, nourish your body with healthy food and water, and get moving as much as possible. Taking these physical steps will make you stronger and more able to take the mental steps necessary to overcome test anxiety.

Review Video: How to Stay Healthy and Prevent Test Anxiety
Visit mometrix.com/academy and enter code: 877894

Mental Steps for Beating Test Anxiety

Working on the mental side of test anxiety can be more challenging, but as with the physical side, there are clear steps you can take to overcome it. As mentioned earlier, test anxiety often stems from lack of preparation, so the obvious solution is to prepare for the test. Effective studying may be the most important weapon you have for beating test anxiety, but you can and should employ several other mental tools to combat fear.

First, boost your confidence by reminding yourself of past success—tests or projects that you aced. If you're putting as much effort into preparing for this test as you did for those, there's no reason you should expect to fail here. Work hard to prepare; then trust your preparation.

Second, surround yourself with encouraging people. It can be helpful to find a study group, but be sure that the people you're around will encourage a positive attitude. If you spend time with others who are anxious or cynical, this will only contribute to your own anxiety. Look for others who are motivated to study hard from a desire to succeed, not from a fear of failure.

Third, reward yourself. A test is physically and mentally tiring, even without anxiety, and it can be helpful to have something to look forward to. Plan an activity following the test, regardless of the outcome, such as going to a movie or getting ice cream.

When you are taking the test, if you find yourself beginning to feel anxious, remind yourself that you know the material. Visualize successfully completing the test. Then take a few deep, relaxing breaths and return to it. Work through the questions carefully but with confidence, knowing that you are capable of succeeding.

Developing a healthy mental approach to test taking will also aid in other areas of life. Test anxiety affects more than just the actual test—it can be damaging to your mental health and even contribute to depression. It's important to beat test anxiety before it becomes a problem for more than testing.

Review Video: Test Anxiety and Depression
Visit mometrix.com/academy and enter code: 904704

Study Strategy

Being prepared for the test is necessary to combat anxiety, but what does being prepared look like? You may study for hours on end and still not feel prepared. What you need is a strategy for test prep. The next few pages outline our recommended steps to help you plan out and conquer the challenge of preparation.

Step 1: Scope Out the Test

Learn everything you can about the format (multiple choice, essay, etc.) and what will be on the test. Gather any study materials, course outlines, or sample exams that may be available. Not only will this help you to prepare, but knowing what to expect can help to alleviate test anxiety.

Step 2: Map Out the Material

Look through the textbook or study guide and make note of how many chapters or sections it has. Then divide these over the time you have. For example, if a book has 15 chapters and you have five days to study, you need to cover three chapters each day. Even better, if you have the time, leave an extra day at the end for overall review after you have gone through the material in depth.

If time is limited, you may need to prioritize the material. Look through it and make note of which sections you think you already have a good grasp on, and which need review. While you are studying, skim quickly through the familiar sections and take more time on the challenging parts. Write out your plan so you don't get lost as you go. Having a written plan also helps you feel more in control of the study, so anxiety is less likely to arise from feeling overwhelmed at the amount to cover. A sample plan may look like this:

- Day 1: Skim chapters 1–4, study chapter 5 (especially pages 31–33)
- Day 2: Study chapters 6–7, skim chapters 8–9
- Day 3: Skim chapter 10, study chapters 11–12 (especially pages 87–90)
- Day 4: Study chapters 13–15
- Day 5: Overall review (focus most on chapters 5, 6, and 12), take practice test

Step 3: Gather Your Tools

Decide what study method works best for you. Do you prefer to highlight in the book as you study and then go back over the highlighted portions? Or do you type out notes of the important information? Or is it helpful to make flashcards that you can carry with you? Assemble the pens, index cards, highlighters, post-it notes, and any other materials you may need so you won't be distracted by getting up to find things while you study.

If you're having a hard time retaining the information or organizing your notes, experiment with different methods. For example, try color-coding by subject with colored pens, highlighters, or post-it notes. If you learn better by hearing, try recording yourself reading your notes so you can listen while in the car, working out, or simply sitting at your desk. Ask a friend to quiz you from your flashcards, or try teaching someone the material to solidify it in your mind.

Step 4: Create Your Environment

It's important to avoid distractions while you study. This includes both the obvious distractions like visitors and the subtle distractions like an uncomfortable chair (or a too-comfortable couch that makes you want to fall asleep). Set up the best study environment possible: good lighting and a comfortable work area. If background music helps you focus, you may want to turn it on, but otherwise keep the room quiet. If you are using a computer to take notes, be sure you don't have any other windows open, especially applications like social media, games, or anything else that could distract you. Silence your phone and turn off notifications. Be sure to keep water close by so you stay hydrated while you study (but avoid unhealthy drinks and snacks).

Also, take into account the best time of day to study. Are you freshest first thing in the morning? Try to set aside some time then to work through the material. Is your mind clearer in the afternoon or evening? Schedule your study session then. Another method is to study at the same time of day that you will take the test, so that your brain gets used to working on the material at that time and will be ready to focus at test time.

Step 5: Study!

Once you have done all the study preparation, it's time to settle into the actual studying. Sit down, take a few moments to settle your mind so you can focus, and begin to follow your study plan. Don't give in to distractions or let yourself procrastinate. This is your time to prepare so you'll be ready to fearlessly approach the test. Make the most of the time and stay focused.

Of course, you don't want to burn out. If you study too long you may find that you're not retaining the information very well. Take regular study breaks. For example, taking five minutes out of every hour to walk briskly, breathing deeply and swinging your arms, can help your mind stay fresh.

As you get to the end of each chapter or section, it's a good idea to do a quick review. Remind yourself of what you learned and work on any difficult parts. When you feel that you've mastered the material, move on to the next part. At the end of your study session, briefly skim through your notes again.

But while review is helpful, cramming last minute is NOT. If at all possible, work ahead so that you won't need to fit all your study into the last day. Cramming overloads your brain with more information than it can process and retain, and your tired mind may struggle to recall even previously learned information when it is overwhelmed with last-minute study. Also, the urgent nature of cramming and the stress placed on your brain contribute to anxiety. You'll be more likely to go to the test feeling unprepared and having trouble thinking clearly.

So don't cram, and don't stay up late before the test, even just to review your notes at a leisurely pace. Your brain needs rest more than it needs to go over the information again. In fact, plan to finish your studies by noon or early afternoon the day before the test. Give your brain the rest of the day to relax or focus on other things, and get a good night's sleep. Then you will be fresh for the test and better able to recall what you've studied.

Step 6: Take a practice test

Many courses offer sample tests, either online or in the study materials. This is an excellent resource to check whether you have mastered the material, as well as to prepare for the test format and environment.

Check the test format ahead of time: the number of questions, the type (multiple choice, free response, etc.), and the time limit. Then create a plan for working through them. For example, if you have 30 minutes to take a 60-question test, your limit is 30 seconds per question. Spend less time on the questions you know well so that you can take more time on the difficult ones.

If you have time to take several practice tests, take the first one open book, with no time limit. Work through the questions at your own pace and make sure you fully understand them. Gradually work up to taking a test under test conditions: sit at a desk with all study materials put away and set a timer. Pace yourself to make sure you finish the test with time to spare and go back to check your answers if you have time.

After each test, check your answers. On the questions you missed, be sure you understand why you missed them. Did you misread the question (tests can use tricky wording)? Did you forget the information? Or was it something you hadn't learned? Go back and study any shaky areas that the practice tests reveal.

Taking these tests not only helps with your grade, but also aids in combating test anxiety. If you're already used to the test conditions, you're less likely to worry about it, and working through tests until you're scoring well gives you a confidence boost. Go through the practice tests until you feel comfortable, and then you can go into the test knowing that you're ready for it.

Test Tips

On test day, you should be confident, knowing that you've prepared well and are ready to answer the questions. But aside from preparation, there are several test day strategies you can employ to maximize your performance.

First, as stated before, get a good night's sleep the night before the test (and for several nights before that, if possible). Go into the test with a fresh, alert mind rather than staying up late to study.

Try not to change too much about your normal routine on the day of the test. It's important to eat a nutritious breakfast, but if you normally don't eat breakfast at all, consider eating just a protein bar. If you're a coffee drinker, go ahead and have your normal coffee. Just make sure you time it so that the caffeine doesn't wear off right in the middle of your test. Avoid sugary beverages, and drink enough water to stay hydrated but not so much that you need a restroom break 10 minutes into the test. If your test isn't first thing in the morning, consider going for a walk or doing a light workout before the test to get your blood flowing.

Allow yourself enough time to get ready, and leave for the test with plenty of time to spare so you won't have the anxiety of scrambling to arrive in time. Another reason to be early is to select a good seat. It's helpful to sit away from doors and windows, which can be distracting. Find a good seat, get out your supplies, and settle your mind before the test begins.

When the test begins, start by going over the instructions carefully, even if you already know what to expect. Make sure you avoid any careless mistakes by following the directions.

Then begin working through the questions, pacing yourself as you've practiced. If you're not sure on an answer, don't spend too much time on it, and don't let it shake your confidence. Either skip it and come back later, or eliminate as many wrong answers as possible and guess among the remaining ones. Don't dwell on these questions as you continue—put them out of your mind and focus on what lies ahead.

Be sure to read all of the answer choices, even if you're sure the first one is the right answer. Sometimes you'll find a better one if you keep reading. But don't second-guess yourself if you do immediately know the answer. Your gut instinct is usually right. Don't let test anxiety rob you of the information you know.

If you have time at the end of the test (and if the test format allows), go back and review your answers. Be cautious about changing any, since your first instinct tends to be correct, but make sure you didn't misread any of the questions or accidentally mark the wrong answer choice. Look over any you skipped and make an educated guess.

At the end, leave the test feeling confident. You've done your best, so don't waste time worrying about your performance or wishing you could change anything. Instead, celebrate the successful completion of this test. And finally, use this test to learn how to deal with anxiety even better next time.

Review Video: 5 Tips to Beat Test Anxiety
Visit mometrix.com/academy and enter code: 570656

Important Qualification

Not all anxiety is created equal. If your test anxiety is causing major issues in your life beyond the classroom or testing center, or if you are experiencing troubling physical symptoms related to your anxiety, it may be a sign of a serious physiological or psychological condition. If this sounds like your situation, we strongly encourage you to seek professional help.

Thank You

We at Mometrix would like to extend our heartfelt thanks to you, our friend and patron, for allowing us to play a part in your journey. It is a privilege to serve people from all walks of life who are unified in their commitment to building the best future they can for themselves.

The preparation you devote to these important testing milestones may be the most valuable educational opportunity you have for making a real difference in your life. We encourage you to put your heart into it—that feeling of succeeding, overcoming, and yes, conquering will be well worth the hours you've invested.

We want to hear your story, your struggles and your successes, and if you see any opportunities for us to improve our materials so we can help others even more effectively in the future, please share that with us as well. **The team at Mometrix would be absolutely thrilled to hear from you!** So please, send us an email (support@mometrix.com) and let's stay in touch.

If you'd like some additional help, check out these other resources we offer for your exam:

http://MometrixFlashcards.com/CSET

Additional Bonus Material

Due to our efforts to try to keep this book to a manageable length, we've created a link that will give you access to all of your additional bonus material.

Please visit http://www.mometrix.com/bonus948/cpacewritten to access the information.